UNLEASH Your Voice

Powerful Public Speaking
for Every Woman

Edited by
Lavinia Thanapathy & Joanne Flinn

PARTRIDGE

To order additional copies of this book, contact
Toll Free 800 101 2657 (Singapore)
Toll Free 1 800 81 7340 (Malaysia)
orders.singapore@partridgepublishing.com

www.partridgepublishing.com/singapore

Coffees and ideas brewed, then pancakes and plans were put on the table over brunch. Seven of us met with a joint vision to make the playing field more equal and bring diversity to stages around the world.

I'm going to succeed, because I'm crazy enough to think I can!

13-5-18

The starting day of a worldwide expansion !

With thanks to the women of vision who planted the seed that grew into this book:
Joyce Carols
Joanne Flinn
Lavinia Thanapathy
Aurelie Saada
Mette Johannson
Kavya Kanchana
Kaumudi Goda

CONTENTS

PART 2: WHAT COMES BEFORE THE TALK

PART 3: WHAT COMES AFTERWARDS:

FOREWORD BY FREDRIK HÄRÉN

My brother was once asked to sit on a panel to discuss the question, "How can we get more women to work in IT?" When he arrived at the panel it turned out that it was an all-male panel. My brother went up on the stage and when he got the first question—"How do we get more women to work in IT?"—he looked out over the audience and said: "I am sure there is a women who can answer that question better than us men. Are there any women in the audience who would like to take my place on the panel?"

Of course there were a bunch of women in the audience who raised their hands, so my brother smiled, stood up, and walked down from the stage to let those women be on the panel instead.

I am telling this story to show the importance of action over words if we want to create a more human society.

As a professional speaker at more than 2,000 conferences in 65 countries around the world over the past 20-plus years, I have always been amazed by the skewed ratio of men to women on stages. When I became the convention chair for the Asia Professional Speakers Convention, a conference for speakers by speakers, I decided to consciously make sure we had equality between male and female speakers. When the convention happened, we did, in fact, have 50/50 male to female speakers. We also had an almost 50/50 split on local to foreign speakers and Asian to non-Asian speakers.

Did we have to work a bit harder to find enough women to put on our short list? Yes. Not because there are not enough great female speakers, but because fewer women raised their hands and applied to speak at the conference. But the important point here is that we did not have to work *so* much harder.

I am both proud and happy we put in the extra time to get a diverse mix of speakers that time, when I was convention chair. But I am surprised—and saddened—when I realized that the reason so many conferences do not have a more diverse mix of speakers is because they choose not to put in that small amount of extra time to make it happen.

A conference with a diverse mix of speakers in regard to background, gender, experience, race, etc., makes a convention more human because it gives more perspectives.

I hope this book will help inspire more conference organizers to make that small extra investment of their time to aim for a more diverse mix of speakers.

And I hope this book will inspire more women to step up and raise their hands to speak at more conferences.

Because audiences want this to happen.

On the world's largest website for speakers, TED.com, 11 out of the 25 most watched speeches are by women! That means 44% of the most popular speeches on the world's most popular site for speeches are by women. In other words, it's naturally almost 50/50. Audiences want to see speeches by women, too. Audiences love speeches from women, too. So, to not offer them women speakers too is simply wrong. And no standards need be lowered to make this shift. As the statistics from TED.com show, when human beings decide what speeches to watch, they do not pick women or men, they pick interesting topics from inspiring speakers. And when they do, almost 50% of them turn out to be women. If that can happen on TED.com, it should happen on conference stages as well.

Fredrik Härén

Fredrik Härén, author of *Spread your message. See the world. How to become a global keynote speaker* and of the blog ProfessionalSpeaking.com

UNLEASH YOUR VOICE

Like all good ideas, this book started on the back of a napkin over brunch. The seven of us at brunch decided to create this book so that more women worldwide could become great professional speakers faster.

Most of the women who have contributed chapters to this book started speaking decades ago. There were even fewer women on stages than there are now. We made the mistakes, stumbled, and got back on our feet. There were no guides to help us. Men were the only role models.

Over time, we've discovered our own voices. We had to learn to unleash our own voices. We found nuances that are powerful for women speakers. We've learned to understand the journey from beginning to speak, to speaking professionally, and then to becoming world-class speakers.

This book is written by TEDx speakers, multi-book authors, and women who have spoken across the world. Some have been interviewed by the BBC, others are Forbes columnists. Some earn their living as speakers, others use speaking to improve their organization or to change the world for the better. These chapters distill our combined 400 years of experience into 14 practical, useful, authentic professional speaking chapters.

This book will ensure that your path to becoming a successful professional speaker will be smoother than ours. This book will give you unique insights into our experiences so that you can learn from our mistakes and our successes.

Why is that important? Public speaking is a crucial component of being able to influence ideas and behaviors on any scale. It is leadership by voice. The way we communicate our ideas touches people, inspires them, and educates and influences their behavior. If we want to be the agents of change in this world, then we need to be able to create change in our own circles of influence. The better our ability to communicate those thoughts, the wider our circle can become.

The book focuses on three key components to successful professional speaking:

- The talk itself: you, the content, your voice, the psychology of a speech, and storytelling
- What comes before the talk: finding your niche, the virtual stage, and building your name and authenticity
- What comes after: getting booked, relationships, negotiating, and the business side of professional speaking

We firmly believe that this is the age of diversity. Now is the time for all of humanity to collaborate, be seen, and heard. Just like we have in this book, women, men and organisations all on the same page. We all have it in our power to close the gender gap in our lifetime, this in turn creates more opportunities for others working towards a more equal future.

The authors of this book have put personal time and money behind it. Many of us are already published authors. We nurtured this book into existence because we all believe that every women needs the tools to be able express their ideas in order to claim their place as leaders in this world.

Each chapter stands on its own. You can read this book from cover to cover or read only the chapters that are relevant to you today. Whether you are presenting to a meeting of three people or to a conference of thousands, there is something here for you. We hope that your copy is dog-eared and filled with markings and notes and that you keep it somewhere on your desk for easy reference and inspiration.

We don't know what the future looks like. But we do know that all of us need to play a part in shaping it. Use your voice. It is how others will hear your ideas and be influenced by them. We wish you every success!

"To all the women who share their voices with the world along with the men who support them."

Lavinia Thanapathy and Joanne Flinn

PART 1

THE TALK ITSELF

This is about you, your content,
your voice, the psychology of
a speech, and storytelling

My Speaking Journey

by Margie Warrell

My first ever public speech was at my children's kindergarten. My nerves were running high and my knees were shaking as my fingers fumbled through the notes I'd brought along as a safety crutch. It's fair to say that I was far more focused on myself—on making a good impression and avoiding making a total fool of myself—than on the people in the room. All three of them.

Needless to say, it was not my finest hour, and I'm grateful that this very humble beginning to my speaker journey was never recorded. In the intervening 15 years I have spoken to thousands of audiences and, yes, my average crowd size has increased. Along the way, I've also learned a great deal about what to do—and perhaps more importantly, about what *not* to do—to engage, inspire, and move an audience, whether of three or three thousand.

One of my most important *aha* moments came one chilly February day in Dallas, Texas, when a tech issue left me without either my slide deck or speaker notes just minutes before I was due to present to about 300 travel industry professionals. Nervous about messing up, I went into the bathroom and said my usual go-to prayer, "Dear God, what do you want me to know?" As always, a divine whisper: "You know your stuff, Margie. You don't need those notes. Just speak to serve and all will be well."

And it was.

In fact, it was the best presentation I'd ever given. More from the heart; less from the head. Which pretty much encapsulates the singular most important ingredient for becoming a truly impactful, and thereby successful speaker: shift your focus from what *you* hope to gain by speaking onto what will most benefit those who will be listening to you.

While "speak to serve" is at the heart of my speaking journey, I've also picked up a few other insights, which I'll outline here. There is no irony in the fact that woven into them is the need for courage. Embracing vulnerability and choosing faith over fear—this is the message that has inspired and shaped the entirety of my life, from picking up my pen to writing my first book to having my fourth child to raising my children around the world while pursuing what I feel is a deep sense of calling.

Speaking from the heart requires living from the heart, and the more you do that in every aspect of your life, the greater your success will be on the stage.

Chart Your Own Path

As the mother of four young children when I first decided to start speaking (initially as a way to build a coaching business), I didn't have much time for professional speaker meetings. However, I recall one that I attended while living in Dallas, where the speaker, a person with lots of speaker credentials, stood on stage and espoused the importance of finding your "signature story," the one story that every speaker needed to define their message and brand and which they would share every time they spoke.

On that suggestion, I wrote down some of the seminal, signature events of my life in an attempt to identify the one that would define my own brand as a speaker. But even my short, short, list had ten life-shaping events. In the end I decided that I was not willing to define myself by just one story. Not only that, I knew that sharing the same story each time I got on stage would bore me stupid. It still does.

I highly recommend that you listen to the advice of such experts but that you apply only what really resonates with you. Forge your own path as a speaker. Never buy into the false belief that someone else's recipe for building a successful speaking career, or even crafting a brilliant keynote, is right for you. If it fits, apply it. If it doesn't, ditch it. Be true to what feels authentic for you and be open to change what you do as you learn and evolve. I have been in a constant state of evolution since I started out, and I have learned more about myself and become more attuned to the hearts of those I speak to.

Be a Thought Leader Who Speaks

I recall being told, early on in my speaker journey, that there are no new ideas in the world, only new ways of sharing old ideas. For instance, I often speak about the importance of taking risks, yet I can hardly claim ownership of the idea that "fortune favors the bold," which predates the Romans. So, I bring my own frameworks, research, and stories to the question of how we can rethink risk in today's overly cautious and uncertain world.

Accordingly, I believe it's often wiser to regard (and brand) yourself as an expert, or "thought leader," who happens to share expertise via speaking, among other ways. If you really want to set yourself apart you need to talk about relevant issues in ways that broaden people's thinking and leave them with insights, ideas, and frameworks that will help them navigate their challenges better. Make time for the deep work of reflective thinking so that you can develop your own body of thought leadership that challenges and expands on the works of other experts. You don't have to reinvent the wheel, but if all you are doing is repeating what someone else has already said then you are limiting the value you bring.

Let Go of Proving Your Brilliance

Early on as a speaker I felt quite insecure about my own worthiness to be in front of an audience, which often left me trying to prove myself and impress them. I'd quote all sorts of research and statistics and share a myriad of models by world renowned experts from prestigious institutions. While I still share research and data where appropriate, I no longer pummel people with them. I've slowly come to realize that when I'm speaking to prove myself, it keeps me from being really present and making the impact I would otherwise make.

I've already mentioned the importance of authenticity, so I won't belabor the point, but the more authentic you are on stage, the more impactful you will be as a speaker. Before people decide what they think of what you have to say, they decide what they think of you. While it's only natural to want people to like you and find you impressive (we're all human!), if your speaking is fueled by an unfilled need to prove your brilliance and worthiness then it undermines your authenticity and will likely trigger a reaction in others that won't serve your cause.

People want to know the human, not the hero. So, find the courage to let go the masks you may want to wear and to just be yourself—real, human, whole-hearted. I can assure you, your message resonates far more deeply when you are willing to trust yourself, to be yourself, and to share your stories of struggle and setbacks rather than just your stories of getting the glory or nailing it the first time.

Risk Rejection, But Don't Over-Personalize It

I have been rejected countless times. By event planners. By speaker bureaus. By (so many) literary agents and media bookers. By HR directors. By book and magazine publishers. By celebrities and experts I've approached to review my books. Even by other not-so-famous speakers and authors who were simply not interested in collaborating or in supporting someone they couldn't see the value of connecting with. Every time this happens I've felt the sting of rejection, if not a rather big kick in the guts. But I've also learned that unless we're willing to risk rejection, we cannot hope to land the opportunities and forge the connections we'd really like.

So, I encourage you to risk those rejections and to put yourself out there, again and again and again. And if at first someone says no, that doesn't mean you can't go back and try again another time. I was knocked back by a leading speaker bureau three times over three years before I finally got them to represent me. Each time I'd go back with another video clip of me speaking or link to a TV interview and then one day, *tada!* (it was a clip from an interview on the *Today Show*). If at first you don't succeed, try, try again. Don't over-personalize the knock-backs—just because someone doesn't appreciate your value doesn't mean you don't have any. And just because they haven't said yes to you *yet* doesn't mean they won't in the future. Keep honing your craft and speaking to serve and let your persistence and passion work their magic.

Start Before You're Ready

I have always been passionate about my speaking subjects, but as I shared at the opening of this chapter, I was not always particularly polished. I doubt even the world's best speakers were brilliant the first time they spoke. My point: don't wait until you're confident you're going to speak with the power of Tony Robbins or the elegance of Oprah before you step onto a platform or speak up in front of a smaller group. You may be waiting your whole life. Rather, give yourself permission not to nail every presentation but to simply to get better at it. Speaking in ways that engage and influence is a skill, and like all skills, you get better at it the more you do it.

Don't Be Too Picky—Or Let Other People Define You!

I remember the first time I was asked how much I charged to give a lunchtime presentation. I'd never charged *anything* up to that point and, honestly, I was pretty thrilled that someone wanted to pay me to speak at all. "Is $200 OK?" I replied a little nervously. Now, you may be shaking your head about how low I priced myself, but the truth is, I was over the moon that someone wanted to pay me $200 for *one hour*. (Like I said, humble beginnings!)

That first paid speaking opportunity came about because I had done several dozen free talks in the preceding year or so in the area where I lived in Dallas, as a way to grow my coaching clientele. I wasn't just new to Dallas, I was new to America, and my network consisted of little more than a few friendly neighbors and other mothers with young kids. Only one woman I knew worked and most the husbands of my female friends saw my coaching as a lovely hobby. Not one ever offered to introduce me to their professional networks. To them I was a stay-at-home mum tinkering in coaching. Thankfully, my husband Andrew was always very encouraging. Time and time again, his belief in me helped me muster up my courage to challenge the rigid gender norms of where I was living and to dare to be more than what so many of those around me—both men and women—expected of me.

Obviously, many people begin their speaker journey with an exponentially stronger network, platform, and level of professional confidence than I had. Hopefully you're one of them! Yet I share this story because I believe that when you are starting out, you need the practice and the exposure even more than you need any income it might provide. The money will come. Even small, free engagements give you the opportunity to develop your thought leadership, hone your craft, cultivate your style, expand your storytelling repertoire, and sharpen your ability to read and engage an audience.

So, while there are some engagements that may simply not be a good fit for you, don't let fees or a false belief that you should be paid every time you speak keep you from seizing opportunities to refine your message or sharpen your skill at sharing it. You have plenty of time to be more selective as word spreads and more people who are in the position to pay hear about how fabulous you are. In the end, my best breaks have come from word-of-mouth recommendations, which all stemmed back to simply showing up to speak.

Build Community

Over the years I've built wonderful friendships with a diverse network of people working in the personal and professional development arena. Some of these people have been focused purely on executive or life coaching, which is where I started out. Others love to stick with facilitating or do nothing but pure keynote speaking. I've learned something from each of them and I value bouncing ideas, sharing resources, and confiding challenges. Every now and again I've encountered people who seem to have viewed me as competition and have held their cards close to their chest. Honestly, these people just aren't my kind of people, as I believe that we are all here to make a difference in our own unique ways and that we all rise by lifting each other. So, be generous in sharing a great resource or connecting people in ways you think would be beneficial to them.

I've now had to start over in three continents, most recently in Asia after moving to Singapore for my husband's career. In Singapore, I've had the privilege of meeting a diverse array of genuine and big-hearted people who've helped me establish a rich network relatively quickly. I encourage you to be proactive in building a diverse network and to be someone others will be grateful to know. Be generous in your support of their development and success. You never know when it will come back your way with some magical opportunity.

Trust Your Intuition

Learning to read the room is a skill that takes time. You build it by simply becoming present to who is sharing your space, putting yourself into their shoes, and tuning into that mystical sixth sense. It's why, when given the opportunity and when my schedule permits, I try to mix with attendees prior to my keynote, even if it's just during a break time. This helps me get a better sense of who I am going to be talking to, rather than stepping on stage blind with only the client briefing as a guide. What do you sense is weighing on people's minds? What emotions are they wrestling with? What unmet needs, frustrations, and fears are standing between them and the actions that would serve them? If you get an inkling, trust it. And then be willing to adjust what you are saying to speak to the concerns and anxieties in the room. On more than one occasion I have replaced a key concept with another one because I felt it was more relevant and accessible for the group. Same for the stories you may share. Sometimes it is better to go with a different anecdote than the one you were planning on. Again, trust your gut to guide you, and you can transform a good speech into a brilliant one.

Embody Your Authority

Your way of being speaks more loudly than your words ever can. So, pay attention to how you show up for others—not just to what you wear or say, but to the presence you bring into the room or onto the stage. Your physiology impacts your psychology. Are you presenting yourself as if you know the value of what you have to say? This isn't about puffing yourself out or putting on a mask of perfection. It's about stepping into your power to embody authority with authenticity, grace, and courage. Remember, this isn't about you.

As I close, three key takeaways.

Three Key Takeaways

- I just want to encourage you to trust whatever it was that called you to want to speak in the first place. The message. The purpose. The compelling why. When you step onto a stage to speak from the heart, it will land on the heart and impact listeners' emotions and the actions they take.
- Embrace the nerves and get comfortable feeling uncomfortable. If it weren't scary, it wouldn't be worth doing.
- Lastly, embrace your setbacks as part and parcel of the process of growing into the woman and speaker you have it within you to become. Don't over personalize them, but learn from them and use them to do better and become braver. You will learn and grow far more from failure than you ever will from success.

Margie Warrell

Hailed as an "international authority on brave leadership" by the *Wall Street Journal*, Margie Warrell draws on her background in business, coaching, and psychology to unleash the potential in organizations from NASA to the UN. Her bestselling books—*Find Your Courage, Stop Playing Safe, Train the Brave, and Make Your Mark*—reflect her passion for helping people to overcome their fear and lead from within.

Margie has gained a wealth of hard-won wisdom about building resilience and cultivating courage since growing up on a small dairy farm in rural Australia. As a mother of four and big sister of seven, she has a special passion for emboldening women to challenge gender norms, embrace their feminine leadership strengths and step into their power as change-makers. The founder of Global Courage and a Women's Economic Forum honoree, she also sits on the advisory board of the Forbes School of Business & Technology. She shares insights from her work and interviews with global leaders such as Richard Branson, Marianne Williamson and Bill Marriott in her Forbes *Courage Works* column.

For more on living and leading with courage: www.MargieWarrell.com

Stage Confidence in Public Speaking

by Lavinia Thanapathy

You've all heard of that infamous study, the one that says that more people are afraid of public speaking than of dying?

I've been doing this for some time now and I can promise you that in all my years of public speaking, no one has actually died from going up in front of an audience and delivering their message.

I understand this is not enough to reassure you. You are probably looking for more substantive help before you get up in front of an audience. Luckily, I have a secret weapon to conquer your fear of public speaking.

The thing is, you're not going to like my secret weapon. It demands time, courage, and commitment.

I'm not going to make you wait till the end of the chapter; I'm going to let you in on it at the start and by the end, you will understand why it is so important.

So, what is it? The secret weapon to make you a confident public speaker is… practice.

Yes, practice. No public speaker became good at their craft without it. The best speakers practice as often as they can. They know that the more they do it, the better they get at it. It is not a skill that you can autopilot through, like cycling. Public speaking is always a conscious effort and the more often you do it, in as many different settings as you can and in front of different audiences, the better you will get.

I will give you tips in this chapter on everything from how to stand to how to dress. But all of what I have to say is worthless unless you commit to practicing. Not just practicing in the safety of your bedroom. No, this secret weapon requires practicing in front of audiences. You can start with your mother if you like and then work your way up and out.

Whether you are a pro speaker looking to refine your technique or a newcomer to public speaking in a panic before addressing a big meeting at your company, this chapter will help you.

Content

Let's start with the easy part. Content is the meat of what you have been asked to speak about. Your content could be world peace, persuading people to be vegans, explaining a science project at school, or presenting a project to your management team at work.

Whether you are addressing the UN or the school PTA, my advice remains the same on content. It works for the world's best speakers and it will work for you.

Stick to three main points or takeaways. Work on your content till you reduce it to only three points for the audience—and for you—to remember.

Keeping your message to three points helps your audience to focus and they have a better chance of remembering what you say. Your audience has a short attention span. You know that already. You are competing with the promise of cute kitten videos on their mobile devices. You know you've lost your audience when more than a third start playing with their phones.

This strategy also helps you to deliver your presentation. If you lose your place, you can easily loop back to your train of thought because you only had three points to make.

Once you've worked out what your message is and how to organize it into three points, you are ready to take your audience on a journey.

This is the fun part. This is the step that means that two speakers on the same topic and with the same three points will influence an audience very differently. This is where you create your differentiator.

Whether you decide to use stories from your own experience, ancient legends, or current affairs, will depend on the audience that you will be delivering your message to.

I speak on diversity and I often tell the story of how I discovered the value of diversity in myself. However, for some audiences, I will choose to use data to make the business case for diversity, rather than the personal case. My choice of which story to tell will depend on the audience and how I think they will need to be persuaded by my message.

Preparation

Perhaps it isn't news to you, but this is the single most important thing you need to know about your presentation: your opening and your closing may be the only two sentences that your audience remembers about what you say.

This means that there are only two sentences that you must be able to deliver while looking into the audience and connecting with them, without glancing at your notes or your slides.

Whatever you do, make your first sentence a powerful one that gets your audience curious about your message.

For instance, when I deliver this chapter as a talk, I might start like this:

"Do you remember the first time that you ever had to face an audience? Perhaps it was your first concert or drama performance at school? Or perhaps it was show and tell at school? Or perhaps it was in front of your team at work? I'd like you take a moment and remember the experience. Did you feel like a deer in headlights? Did your mouth go dry? Did your mind go blank? Did you suddenly feel an urgent need to pee? Did you freeze? Or did you thoroughly enjoy the experience and decide instantly that this was your future career?"

And that's really all I have to remember. The rest of it comes from the story journey that I have built for the audience. But those first lines must be delivered without looking at my notes or slides, spoken to the audience like it's the first time I have ever said it, and like each audience member is the only person in the room. The story journey is a courtship. Make the first impression count.

In order to do this, you need to know who your audience is. The more specific the better. Even if the audience demographic is varied, work out what their commonality is. All women? Mostly engineers? All parents? Mostly people who have anxiety about public speaking? The more you know, the more satisfying and successful the courtship will be.

I was at a conference once and one of the keynote presenters had sent a survey out to the audience to find out what they wanted him to talk about. It was no surprise that his keynote was well received, as he had targeted his talk to what the audience wanted. I myself have never done this, but I have always asked for an audience brief from the event organizer and I always try to speak to the organizer in advance to get as much information as possible about the audience.

Why is it so essential to know about your audience? Because this will help you answer the most important question when you are crafting your content: what does the audience need to walk away with, intellectually and emotionally, from our encounter?

Understanding the intellectual takeaway helps you work out what information or knowledge you need to impart. Knowing the emotional component will decide the type of journey you need to take them on to impart that knowledge. Don't ignore the second part. It's the thing women are most intuitive about and often suppress. Let your antenna work its magic.

When I deliver this chapter in person, the audience needs practical techniques to make them better public speakers (intellectually) and they need to be persuaded (emotionally) that they can do this and that it's not too hard for them.

Once you balance this intellectual/emotional approach, your three-point content will fall into place.

And you can test it. Invite someone who fits your audience demographic to coffee and casually discuss your topic with them. Watch for their reactions and listen to their point of view. This will help you refine your presentation for content and tone. I also do this to test the effect of stories that I want to tell during the presentation. Watch closely for body language and other signals in addition to whatever feedback the person gives you verbally.

For instance, I might be speaking on diversity to a professional women's group or to government policy makers. The points I make are obviously very different for each group, and what works with one group might not work with the other. This is especially important for keynote speakers. Always find a way to test your message, especially if you are presenting in front of a new crowd.

Delivery

If you are asked to speak on a topic or you've offered to do a talk, the most important thing you need is to believe that you are the best person for the job. You are the reason people will turn up. They want to hear you speak about your topic. Your point of view is important. Your job is to make it persuasive so that you can influence change.

You are the right person for your topic, so don't apologize for your presence. I see so many people, particularly women, apologize for being the person delivering the message. Self-deprecation does not belong on a professional stage. It works well for stand-up comedians, but I'm going to guess that's not your line of work if you are reading this book.

If you want to persuade and influence, you need to be able to present your ideas in a way that leads your audience to your point of view. You cannot do that if you don't think you know what you are talking about.

> You: I like what I see.
> Audience: What do you see?
> You: Sorry, but my eyesight is failing. I'm not really sure what I see.
> Audience: [changes the channel]

Don't get in front of an audience till you believe the following things. You are the best person to deliver this message to this audience. You can create change with your message. You can influence thoughts with your message. Your ideas are worth people's time and attention.

Don't shrink on stage. Don't giggle. Don't apologize. Start with your voice low and loud and speak slowly and clearly when you say your first words. Research shows that audiences of both genders attribute authority to a lower tone and pitch. With our naturally higher range, women start at a disadvantage on this score. Don't make it worse by going even higher up on the range because you are nervous.

The best thing to do is to consciously say your first sentence, slowly and in a tone that is one notch lower than how you naturally speak. Practice this during the sound check; use your first sentence to test the mic. Say it the first time in your usual tone and then lower your tone and say it again. This lower tone is what you will start your talk with.

Also, make sure you get the audience's attention by being a notch louder than usual. I see too many people, both men and women, make this fundamental mistake at the start of their talk. They put so much effort into crafting a strong start and they don't deliver it loudly enough for the audience to hear them. Always start a little louder than usual. You can settle into your natural volume and pitch as you go along, but always get the audience's attention first. This gives them a chance to focus on you.

Appearance

For women in particular, the question of what to wear on stage is a particularly fraught one. Men seem to manage with a dark suit and a pop of color from their choice of tie. There are lessons here for us, too.

Not the dark suit—that wastes the one benefit of being a woman on stage. We get to stand out visually even before we say a single word. Don't squander that opportunity.

Of course, if black is your brand color then stay true to it. But if you are wearing black because of the misguided idea that it will make you look slimmer or help reduce wardrobe pain, then please reconsider.

We are not chameleons. Our purpose on a stage is not to blend into the background. One of the questions to ask when you get your speaker's brief is what color the backdrop will be. Then choose a color that will allow you to stand out against that backdrop.

I always recommend that you wear a bright color. Have you seen what TV anchorwomen wear? They almost never wear all black, and they usually have an extremely bright pop of color somewhere on their outfit. I suggest you watch the news on different channels to see what female anchors are wearing and then adapt something that works for you.

I have a "uniform" of sorts that I always wear when I'm speaking on stage or on TV. What works for me is black, tailored pants/trousers with pockets, a black shirt/t-shirt/camisole, and a brightly colored, tailored jacket. I always wear solid heels, not stilettos. I never wear anything new for the first time on stage, especially not shoes. I wear a two-piece outfit with a jacket so that I have somewhere to hook a battery pack for a lapel mic. You don't want to find yourself in the position of having to hold a clicker for your presentation in one hand and the battery pack in the other because you are wearing a dress with no pockets.

I never wear skirts or dresses on stage, but that is a personal decision. I know many successful women speakers who only wear skirts or dresses onstage. Just be aware of the length of your hemline and always check in the mirror to see how high the hemline will ride when you sit down. This decision is less important if your presentation is to be delivered standing, but always take into account the angle of the stage when deciding to wear a skirt or dress.

This is an especially important consideration for seated panel discussions. The audience is almost always looking at knee height and a skirt or dress riding up will distract both you and the audience from your message. Increasingly, I have been offered a bar stool rather than an armchair for panel discussions and I know that I cannot manage a bar stool with a skirt. If you can without doing a Sharon Stone, then more power to you. I caution against this though—and remember to check for yourself against a full-length mirror.

I know many women rely on a statement necklace or earrings to jazz up their ensemble. I myself have an extensive collection of these. Whatever you choose, make sure that your jewelry will not move onstage. If it is likely to sway or jingle or make any sound or movement, it does not belong on a professional speaking stage. I've seen women speakers have to remove necklaces that kept hitting their lapel mics.

The same rule applies if you are wearing your national dress onstage. Many successful women speakers do this and it can make a wonderful impact, especially if your topic is tied to your culture or tradition. Once again, the no-movement rule applies. As an Indian, my national dress is a saree. I only wear it when I act as Master of Ceremonies gala dinners and I always have it pinned into place. I also drape it a little higher off the ground so I won't trip if I have to go up and down the stage.

Even for the most glamourous of events, I will never wear strappy evening shoes onstage. The rest of my outfit may fit the glamour of the context, but my shoes will always be comfortable court shoes with a solid heel that I am unlikely to slip out of, snap, or trip over. I cannot over-emphasis the role that shoes play in grounding your presence on stage. I strongly discourage thin heels of any sort. Find flats or heels with some substance. Wear your shoes regularly so they will not pinch onstage. The shoes you wear on stage must *never* be new and never be uncomfortable. When you stand in them, you must feel like you can tackle anything in them.

You may already have a well-established brand for yourself or for the organization that you represent. This may require you to always wear red, khaki shorts, an evening dress, a flapper skirt, or even all black. If this is the established brand that you represent, then stay true to it. My advice on shoes stands regardless.

Stage Presence

Few things have influenced my speaking more than Amy Cuddy's 2012 TED Talk. She speaks about faking it till you make it by adopting a power pose for two minutes, to give yourself the confidence that you might not be feeling. I strongly encourage any public speaker to watch this talk.

I practice it this way. When I arrive at my speaking venue, I first check out the stage. I will ask someone to take a full-length photo of me on the stage. I check that my outfit works with the backdrop. Then I do a sound check, and finally I go to the bathroom with my phone. I set a timer for two minutes and I do the Wonder Woman pose in the privacy of the bathroom cubicle. If you have a green room, even better. But use whatever the venue has. You have to try this strategy to know what an amazing impact it will have on your presence.

I prefer not to use a rostrum or a table on stage because I dislike any barrier between myself and my audience. However, in some circumstances this is unavoidable. If you have rostrum, make yourself as comfortable behind it as you can. If you are petite, ask for a step so you can see the audience. If you are tall, make sure that the mic is not too far away to pick up your voice. Do *not* grip the sides of the rostrum. Stay close to the rostrum and the mic and rest your hands on it. It is unlikely that the audience will see any low hand gestures, so if it is important for you to use your hands while you talk, make sure your hands are above the edge of the rostrum.

Ideally, I like to stand in the center of the stage or space. I will adjust to the side to accommodate a projector or other presentation device, but my preference is to be centered. Many women stand to one side of the stage even when there is no projector or slides. Don't do this. If you are speaking, take center stage. Standing to the side will not make you more persuasive; it just makes the audience strain to see you.

When you stand, keep your legs about the same distance apart as your shoulders. Hold your hands at your sides and bent at about a 90-degree angle. Keep your elbows close to your body unless you are making a deliberate gesture. Stake your claim to the stage and hold your ground. Take a few seconds to ground yourself before you start. It's perfectly fine to stand silently on stage for a few seconds before you begin, looking out into the crowd. This will help you command your audience's attention *before* you start.

I often get asked how much movement is expected from a speaker. My answer is that in most cases, your movement is directly correlated to the length of the presentation. If you are speaking for under 15 minutes, don't pace the length of the stage or room. Imagine a circle of about a meter around you and stick to occupying that space. You will exhaust your audience if you bounce about wildly for a short presentation. You want them to focus on your words.

If you are speaking at length, say for 30–60 minutes or longer, changing your position on stage or even moving into the audience or around the room is helpful in keeping your audience engaged. Move when you are making a new point or changing the format; this kind of deliberate movement helps the audience refocus at key moments and keeps their minds from wandering off.

Practice

Remember our secret weapon? All this advice will only benefit you if you put it into practice by *practicing*. You cannot get better unless you are speaking in front of other people.

Start small. Speak in front of your husband, mother, sibling, best friend, or class. It really doesn't matter how small the audience is—you need it to practice. You can do a test run in front of your mirror or a video camera, but to get better you need a real-life audience.

Accept free speaking opportunities wherever you find them. Choose some low-risk, friendly audiences. Join a toastmaster's group if that works for you.

I practiced by speaking in front of the professional women's group that I belonged to. I got so good that I even became president of the group. And because I got so many requests to speak, the group started a professional women's speaking registry. Start small if you need to. You will get more comfortable and you will get better. Your steps can be any size you need. Take leaps when you feel ready. Challenge yourself. You will be surprised by how quickly you will improve.

Three Key Takeaways

- You are the best person to deliver your keynote. You are there to persuade and to influence. Know your audience and work out what your audience needs to hear from you, both intellectually and emotionally.
- Work out a uniform for your presentations that is comfortable and suits you. Never wear anything that is new or that moves on stage, and always wear comfortable shoes. Do not shrink on stage. Occupy your space with confidence. Do a power pose for two minutes before you go on stage.
- Practice. Practice. Practice. This is the real secret to being a great public speaker.

Lavinia Thanapathy

Lavinia Thanapathy is the Chair of Inspiring Girls Singapore and Vice President at the Singapore Council for Women's Organizations. She is passionately committed to creating an equal future through the empowerment of women and girls. A lawyer by training and a branding expert by profession, Lavinia has served as Honorary Secretary at HCA Hospice Care and was a three-term President at the PrimeTime Business & Professional Women's Association. In addition to her board roles, Lavinia speaks on issues around gender diversity at organizations like the World Intellectual Property Organization, DHL, and Google. She is also a sought-after media commentator on issues around women and leadership.

For more on empowering women and leadership:
www.LaviniaThanapathy.com

The Tear and 10,000 – Using The Power of Data and Visuals

by Joanne Flinn, the Business Growth Lady

When I was a child, I was surrounded by scientists. My dad was one. Data, statistics, and math were part of the normal language of my world. I learned it a bit like I learned English—with touches of slang from friends and accents from other parts of the world.

It was only when I was at university, when I got through first-year math with the engineers and science students, that I realized I was a little different. I was studying business, economics, and law, not science like the rest of them.

I was also different in that I was a girl who was comfortable with numbers, who was fine with statistics, who knew the power of data.

I'm also a human being and an artist. At 50, after having done the responsible adult business career, part of me was screaming inside. I'd ignored it for over 25 years. Eventually, I listened. This journey ended up as a TEDx Talk, "When Art Meets Logic." Between you and me, I was terrified of showing up as the real me. If you watch the talk, you'll see how I pause just as I begin to talk about the deeper truths of me. Those pauses for breath were for courage. These days the artist me now shows up alongside my business/scientist self.

Your talk will need both art and logic. They are powerful forces.

Stories are super powerful, and visuals are too. They connect with part of our humanity. Numbers, data, and math connect to a different part of us.

In this chapter, I'm going to show you how to add strength to your impact, story, and keynote with numbers and visuals in a seven-step process.

As for the tear, I'll tell you about that later.

STEP 1: What's Your Goal?

Do you need data or statistics or numbers? Some of you reading this will say, "But my topic is about the human side of things, about feelings or art." Whether or not you need statistics depends on who you wish to influence and the purpose of your message.

If your aim is purely to share a personal story, perhaps not. If your point is that key elements of the story have a broader application, then data helps to show that this is so.

For example:

> *Bob has a debilitating disease. He's housebound and unable to walk to the bus or work. His family is struggling. He's depressed, unable to contribute. There are 15,000 Bobs in our city alone.*

Citing those 15,000 Bobs shows the broader view on your subject.

STEP 2: Understand Your Audience

Consider your audience. If your audience consists of data-oriented people, such as scientists, engineers, design thinkers, business people, or policy folk, then data is necessary for credibility.

For example:

> *13% of the stock market value is physical and financial assets, while 87% of the current stock market value is based on non-traditional capital.*

You can put it in a slide like this:

Number as a statement

Or like this:

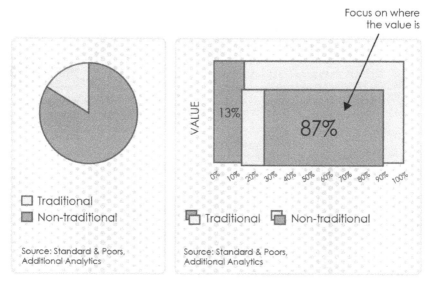

Pie charts or stacks use highlights to draw attention

As I have done here, include your source. All data has sources. Credit them or you'll be discredited in the eyes of your data-minded audience.

Data has excellent myth-busting capacity. Data is a useful way to help people reframe their perception, from "I think it is like this because that's what I've heard," to, "Oh, this is how it really is."

STEP 3: Design Your Narrative Journey

Consider where your listeners are and where you want them to go.

As you put your talk together, get data, and get it from as credible a source as you can. Do your research.

Does your data support your argument and direction? Is it something you need to know or to respond to? Consider the information that those in the room will bring with them. What can you build on or add? What will you need to reframe or correct? What is the narrative journey you'll take them on?

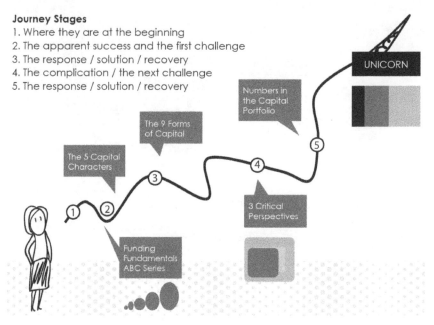

Journey Stages
1. Where they are at the beginning
2. The apparent success and the first challenge
3. The response / solution / recovery
4. The complication / the next challenge
5. The response / solution / recovery

Credit: Underlying structure is Joseph Campbell's Hero's Journey

A narrative journey — draw one for your talk

STEP 4: What Will Help This Journey?

Consider where data and visuals will help your audience on their journey. Determine three data points and three emotions and the visuals that reflect these.

Data helps to tell a complex story in simple terms. For example:

> *Why raise capital? It helps you to expand the size of the pie so the slice you have is bigger.*

> This sounds logical. But you need a visual to help drive it home. In this case, use a visual built in two steps:

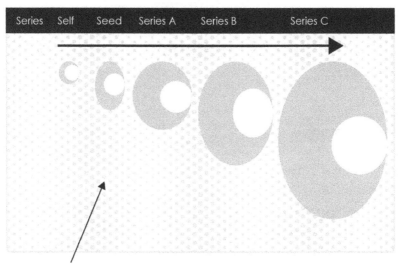

Visual to achor the story logic

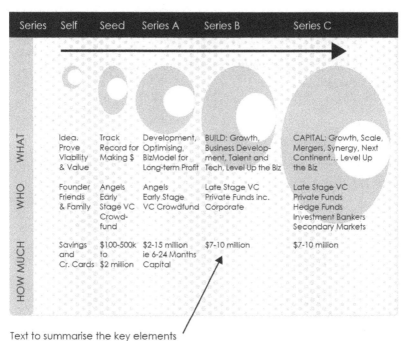

Text to summarise the key elements

Think about the photos audience members will take.
The visual helps them recall your message.

Build the visuals and text

You may want to lay out a progressive set of complications. For example:

50 years ago, a law was passed that said equal work for equal pay.

However, in 2018, women are paid 24% less than men, on average.

Over a lifetime, she'll earn 57% of a man's earnings.

At retirement, she'll have saved $641,000 less than a man with the same career path.

She'll live longer on less.

This is more than a challenge for an individual across a lifetime. It's more than the fact that this affects the 50% of humanity that is female and their children, both boys and girls.

It's that the 2035 Sustainable Development Goals for the health of our planet have identified that economic equity is critical to the achievement of all other goals in the next 17 years.

And yet research by the World Economic Forum finds that at current rates of progress it will take 217 years to reach economic equity.

That's 200 years too late. This is the purple elephant in the room. Economic equity is a challenge for humanity to answer successfully swiftly, and not simply for women's sake.

You can support your audience's journey through the data with thoughtful slides. For example:

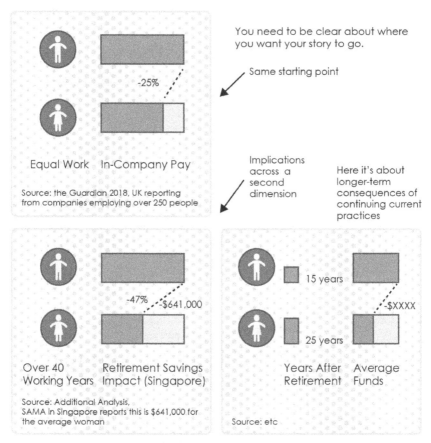

Graphics help support and build your story for your audience

STEP 5: Consider the Human Learning Journey

For many people, straight numbers are not so easy to relate to. Graphics help. Here is the same story with the data illustrated. In this case, I've decided to lead the audience to a different point.

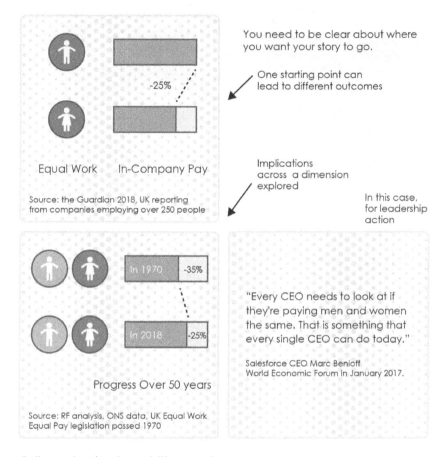

You need to be clear about where you want your story to go.

One starting point can lead to different outcomes

-25%

Equal Work   In-Company Pay

Source: the Guardian 2018, UK reporting from companies employing over 250 people

Implications across a dimension explored

In this case, for leadership action

In 1970   -35%

In 2018   -25%

"Every CEO needs to look at if they're paying men and women the same. That is something that every single CEO can do today."

Salesforce CEO Marc Benioff
World Economic Forum in January 2017.

Progress Over 50 years

Source: RF analysis, ONS data, UK Equal Work Equal Pay legislation passed 1970

Retirement savings impact (Singapore)

You may find the story works best over several slides

You'll use data to support your structure, as part of the framework. You may choose not to refer to it during your talk, but it adds to your background substance. Remember, professional speakers have data even if they don't use it. Think about how you might depict it so that it tells the story you are after.

Consider where you need graphics to support your data or even photographs to make and support the emotional point that you are making. A simple, powerful photograph will contribute a lot to the story you are telling.

Visuals and graphics help people get a sense of relationships and quantification. Color helps with focus.

For example, while the graphics in this book are in gray tones, notice how white has been used to highlight, while black is used to create depth. The grays are mid-tones that tell the bulk of the story.

Reds, yellows and oranges are warm and move forward toward the viewer, while blues are cool and recede. Greens and purples vary depending on their red/blue tones. Colors have a huge impact on people's perceptions.

If you can, pick a brand template for your colors, graphics, and style.

Andrea Edwards uses Roy Lichtenstein-inspired pop art in her graphics. These are instantly recognizable as Andrea's brand in social posts. Sonja Piontek uses a few powerful words and a single image as part of her clean German style. I use clean graphics as well as dramatic images that reflect the emotional tone of what I'm speaking about, which aligns with my brand as someone who lives both logic and art. You'll recognize the influence of both Andrea's style and my style in this book's graphics.

Pick images that are clear, high resolution, and aligned to both your brand and your story. People remember visuals. They'll photograph them. Great ones may go viral.

Photo Credit: Sarah Rixom

A picture doing 1,000 words in a moment

You can change the emotional tone in the room in under a second with your visuals.

STEP 6: Simplify

Review your data and visuals and see how much you can take out or hide. Statistics and slides are good scaffolding, they are great support to a powerful keynote. However, keep the number of slides that you actually display to a minimum. Every time you put a slide up or change a slide, your audience's attention moves from you to the slide. It reduces the connection between them and you. Be really deliberate about when the slide adds to your audience's journey and where it might distract.

When you change slides, pause and give your audience a moment to absorb the visuals and data.

STEP 7: REHEARSE!

Visuals and data are now props and support tools for your speech. Know your slides and the key messages of them so well that you can simply click forward. Turning to check or look at the slide disconnects you from the audience. Know your topic and the slides so well you stay connected, and trust that your preparation has you tuned into your topic, its nuances, and your audience's bigger needs.

These seven steps help you combine art and science to add depth, richness, and impact to your talk. The architecture of the journey helps you navigate between story and data, between challenges and solutions, between insight and impact.

Three Key Takeaways

- Have data and do your research.
- Know your audience and design your data and visuals to support their journey.
- Use data and visuals as scaffolding to help your talk create the impact and action you intend.

Reminder: Credit your sources on data, visuals, and photographs.

And the tear and the 10,000?

You've heard a picture is worth a thousand words, right? When you connect through your heart to your audience and you have good data, graphics, and visuals, you are a powerful speaker. As you walk off stage, you may just get a tear of joy in your eye, and feel, "Yes, I did it. I made an impact today." I hope you do.

You may also find these resources useful:

- Hans Rosling's TED Talk, "The Best Stats You've Ever Seen"
- Dan Roam's superb book *The Back of the Napkin*
- Unsplash for free images and photos
- Upwork and Fiver for freelance graphic designers who can transform data into visuals

Joanne Flinn

Joanne Flinn, the Business Growth Lady, is an international award-winning author, futurist, and board director. She ran her first $10 million business at 24, before going on to lead multi-million-dollar businesses for PricewaterhouseCoopers. Founder and CEO of Project Wings Pte. Ltd. Joanne helps leaders grow their business bringing together capital, digitisation, creativity, and people. She's spoken across the globe at leading industry conferences, twice at TEDx and is part of the Oxford Futures Forums at the University of Oxford's Saïd Business School. Joanne is the Founder of the Purple Elephant movement on the power of gender pay equity to create a better world. A true post-modern renaissance artist, she has exhibited under the name Booth Aster in the USA, Spain, Germany and at the ArtScience Museum in Singapore as TEDx Artist-In-Residence.

For more on growth, equity and the human side of the future: www.JoanneFlinn.com

Voice and Presence

by Cynthia Zhai

Introduction

There is no sound more powerful than your speaking voice. It is through your voice that you stir thoughts, evoke emotions, and inspire actions. Your voice is your most powerful tool as a speaker. It can make or break your connection with the audience the moment you open your mouth to speak. It can motivate or demoralize your audience. It can move your audience into action or let them stay indifferent.

If you want to influence your audiences and make a difference in their lives, you can't overlook this powerful tool, your voice.

What Is It?

Voice is vibration. It originates in the vibration on your vocal cords, powered by your breath, amplified by the cavities in your body and given meaning by the use of articulators. Working on your voice means working on that vibration. When your vibration is optimized, you become more magnetic as a speaker.

Voice is energy. When you use your voice, there's a flow of energy going through your body. When your voice is stuck, so is your energy. Working with your voice means breaking through the blockages of energy in your body. When energy starts to flow in your body, you attract rather than repel your audience.

You are your voice. A breath of air flows into your body, taking on your unique thoughts, feelings and emotions, and when it re-emerges it shows to the world who you are. When you develop your voice, you develop your authenticity.

What Do Professional Speakers Sound Like?

Great professional speakers have developed their voices. When they speak, they are magnetic, authentic, and influential.

1. Magnetic

Great speakers are magnets. They draw their audiences in with a magnetic voice and personality. Audiences hang on every word they say, see them as role models, and become their biggest fans.

Great speakers have worked on themselves. They strive to be the embodiment of what they have to say. When they speak, it is not only their words but who they are that is magnetic.

2. Authentic

Great speakers have found their authentic voice, literally and metaphorically.

There are no two voices alike. One may be able to impersonate a celebrity's voice, but nuances such as the texture, stability or instability, fullness or the lack of fullness, and so on, cannot be replicated. Indeed, voice reflects who you are.

Great speakers are not afraid of being vulnerable in front of their audiences. They know it is their vulnerability that makes them human and inspires audiences. They don't see themselves as gurus but as relatable human beings who have just walked one step ahead of their audiences.

A great speaker friend of mine once said, "I'm not an inspirational speaker. I'm an inspired speaker." My friend's authenticity and humility have inspired so many people.

3. Influential
Great speakers' voices stir thoughts and evoke emotions. They are able to influence their audiences and that influence lasts far longer than the speech they give. Audiences take their advice and change their own lives for the better.

What Do World-Class Speakers Sound Like?

What separates world-class speakers from the rest is that they take a stand, they fight for a cause, and they are on a mission.

World-class speakers are the movers and shakers of our time. They are not afraid of judgement when they take a stand. They are not afraid of speaking their mind when they fight for a cause. They are not afraid of rejection when they are on a mission. Judgement, fear, and rejection are not considered at all.

Malala is a world-class speaker, and world-class speakers don't set limits on themselves. Malala started speaking her mind when she was only 11 years old. She was not afraid to take her stand and fight for girls' education; she continued to speak her mind after she was shot by a Taliban gunman. She's on a mission.

Aung San Su Kyi is a world-class speaker.[1] Despite multiple arrests, she spoke her mind against the brutal ruling of the dictator in Myanmar. She could have chosen to leave the country for her freedom, but she chose to stay in her country under house arrest for years to fight for what she believed in.

World-class speakers do not need a stage to move and shake our society. Every interaction, every statement, and every action is a speech of deep impact.

What Have I Learned?

1. It is not about being liked
It is in women's DNA that we want to be liked. In the Stone Age, if a woman was not liked it equaled to death. She would be thrown out of the tribe and would never survive on her own.

I wanted to be liked and accepted by every audience member when I started out as a speaker. I wouldn't say things that I thought people would disagree with. I wouldn't point out their real problems in fear of creating conflict with them. In the end, I wasn't making a difference. I was just another regular speaker.

It was not until I got over my fear of being disliked, fear of being rejected, and fear of conflict that I started to stir thoughts and make a real difference in the lives of my audiences.

2. Dare to take a stand
When we want to be liked, we don't dare to rock the boat and take a stand.

It can be unsettling and risky getting a lot of attention, which carries the potential for judgement and rejection. Tell me about it. I was the one who used to be so worried about judgement and rejection. Then I had this revelation: to take a stand is not about you. That's right. It's for a bigger purpose. It's to change the world, one opinion, one person, one speech at a time.

There's no one better than a professional speaker to take a strong stand, to speak their mind, and to move and shake the world.

3. Be unapologetically you
We are living in a world that's overloaded with information.

There are over 1.8 billion websites on the internet, according to the Netcraft 2018 Web Server Survey.

More than 400 hours of video is uploaded to YouTube every single minute. That's the statistic as of July 2015! YouTube has yet to release the latest figures on uploads, but it's safe to imagine much more than 400 hours.

We are bombarded by information every day, so ask yourself, when you give a speech, "Why would people listen to me?"

They listen to you not because you have important information to share. With a touch of a finger, they could find more information online than you could ever present in 30 minutes. They could walk out of the room to watch a Youtube video and the presenter on Youtube may be much more interesting than you are. Ouch—it hurts.

The world craves fresh ideas and is obsessed with creativity and innovation. However, creativity and innovation don't mean being different on purpose. Having something to say isn't about when the crowd is saying yes and you choose to say no, just to be different.

It took me a deep learning curve to realize what the world needs is for us to look within and search for what we believe in and what makes us unique: you; your story, your experience, your struggles, the lessons you learned, and everything about you. This is the time we need your authentic voice.

You are not a messenger. You are the message.

What Do Women Speakers Need to Consider?

Don't be afraid to stand out. Most of us women want to be liked and want to fit in. Standing out and being too individualistic is seen as ambitious, aggressive, and selfish, so we dim our light.

When we dim our light, we don't serve anyone. It is in our difference that we serve.

In a world of information explosion, we don't need another voice to bore us with information that we can find on the internet.

At a moment when people in the world are losing trust,[2] we need women, who are traditionally seen as more trustworthy than men, to take a stand and speak their minds.

This is the time we need women's authentic voices and expert perspectives to stand as the authority.

Be vulnerable
To succeed in male-dominated working environments, many women have muscled up with masculine energy and tucked away their vulnerability.

In a world dominated by masculine energy, it is all about getting things done and making things happen. Thus we lack warmth, nurturing, compassion, and intuition—the feminine energy that makes the world a blissful place to live in.

As women speakers we need to bring our gifts to the world, the feminine energy to complement the dominant masculine energy. It is in our vulnerability as well as our logic that we relate to the audience, touch their hearts, and inspire them into action.

I walk into a room
Just as cool as you please,
And to a man,
The fellows stand ...
. . . .
I say,
It's the fire in my eyes,
. . . .
I'm a woman,
Phenomenally.
—Maya Angelou[3]

What I Wish I Had Known Earlier

I wish I had better understood the differences between masculine energy and feminine energy, and known that we need them in equal parts in our pursuit of world class and success.

We made ourselves look strong, speak with logic, and put our emotions aside until we found that the old masculine way of doing things wasn't working, and until we found ourselves stressed and unfulfilled.

I wish I had learned earlier to appreciate the power of feminine energy. I wish I could have listened to my intuition earlier. I wish I could have undressed the masculine energy wrapped around me earlier.

A friend of mine likes to say, "Leave your two balls at home." It is a rough saying and it is a hard truth. Use your feminine, caring energy in speaking and growing your speaking business, rather than selling, up-selling, and cross-selling.

What It Takes to Develop Your Voice and Your Presence

You are your voice. Your voice reflects who you are. When you've developed your voice, you become whole, authentic, and magnetic. Your confidence will soar and your influence will grow.

Here are four key essentials that help you find your voice and develop yourself into more whole, authentic, and magnetic speaker.

- **Relaxation**
  Tension is the enemy of your voice. To speak with a magnetic voice, you must learn how to release tension in your body. For example, tension in your jaw makes you mumble or sound nasal. Tension could also make your voice tremble or go high-pitched when you are nervous on stage.

  Relaxation can release unnecessary tension in your body and keep it from hindering proper voice projection. Relaxation is not about getting loose or floppy. Neither does it require working too hard. It is achieved when you balance making an effort and letting go. It requires you to free your mind from any thought and focus on every movement you are making; it requires you to engage in the necessary effort and allow yourself to be led by that effort.

  One of the easiest ways to achieve a quick release of tension is to sigh. Sighing seems simple, yet its effects are profound. A sigh of relief is one of the secrets to making your voice effortless.

  When you sigh, you let go. When you speak, you let go. When you project your most powerful voice, you let go. There's no effort anywhere in your body. The most powerful voice comes from the least effort.

Start sighing before you project your voice, and before you practice the next two steps.

- **Breathing**

    Breath is the power of your voice. It determines the quality of your voice. The quality of your voice will never exceed the quality of your breath. To have a magnetic voice, you must learn how to breathe properly and fully.

    You may have heard people say, "To improve your voice, you need to breathe from your diaphragm."

    First of all, there's no such thing as breathing from the diaphragm. When we inhale the air goes into our lungs and when we exhale the air comes out. We breathe from the lungs, not the diaphragm. In fact, the diaphragm is only a piece of muscle that supports proper breath.

    For proper breathing, the diaphragm should move down and out when we inhale. As a result, you see your stomach move out. When you exhale, the stomach will move in.

    That's the opposite of what you've been doing for the past 21 years (if you're forever 21 like the rest of us). To change the inefficient way you've been breathing, you'll need to practice breathing exercises on a daily basis until proper breathing becomes a habit. Only when proper breathing becomes a habit will you be able to speak with a calm and powerful voice even if you still feel nervous.

    Kungfu Breathing, an exercise I designed, is one of the easiest exercises you can practice to correct your breathing. Breathe in fully through an open mouth. Then push your stomach in to propel the air out through your mouth. Once your breath has been pushed out, you should feel an urge to take another breath in. This next inhalation is often a proper breath and you'll feel your stomach coming out naturally. Then repeat the process a few times.

This exercise forces you to engage your diaphragm and is the most effective exercise to help you form the correct breathing habits. While this exercise doesn't represent how you are going to breathe normally, it's very useful for retraining your diaphragm muscle to move properly.

You'll notice you breathe through the mouth in this Kungfu Breathing exercise. This is important. When your mouth is open, you are more relaxed; an open mouth allows air to come in and out more easily.

Practice this exercise for a minute or two at a time, six to eight times a day. For the first 45 to 60 days, practice this exercise consistently. In your daily normal breathing you don't need to practice anything, but before you know it, proper breathing will become a habit.

- **Resonance**
Resonance is the amplification of your voice through vibrations in your body. It is resonance that gives your voice depth, fullness, and richness. Resonance is the secret to a more magnetic and authentic voice. It is also the key to finding your balance and alignment physically, mentally, emotionally, and spiritually.

Resonance is impossible to achieve without proper breathing as a habit. For this reason, you should only practice resonance exercise after 45 to 60 days of breathing practice as outlined above.

One relatively easy exercise to practice resonance is to make a *hmm* sound when you breathe out. Take a full breath in, and notice your stomach come out if you breathe properly. When you exhale, as your stomach moves in, make the *hmm* sound.

When you feel this vibration in your whole body, you know you are developing resonance.

Practice this exercise for a minute or two at a time, six to eight times a day for forty-five to sixty days.

- **Color**

  Color is what gives your voice life. It makes what you say come alive and it helps you engage and inspire. To speak with color is not just to vary your pitches, tonalities, volume levels, or pacing. If you focus on these aspects of speaking, you'll come across as incongruent and inauthentic.

  To have different colors and shades in your voice is to speak with a voice that's expressive, engages your audiences, and touches them on a deeper level, through authentic expression.

Whether you are an introvert or extrovert, you have an authentic voice inside of you. You can uncover that voice and let it reflect the depth in you and the shades of your character.

You don't need to—and you simply can't—speak with a voice that doesn't feel right. If you try to do so, your whole life will feel like it's not right.

When you stay true to your inner voice you will feel liberated to speak your truth.

A client of mine, whom I'll call Fay, is an introvert. When she spoke, she found her voice monotonous and uninteresting. She felt that she couldn't make the impact she knew she wanted to in her listeners' lives.

During our work together, Fay was very proactive and diligent with her practicing. But something didn't feel right in the way she practiced. It turned out that when she wanted to sound colorful, she would put on a "radio voice" that was clearly not her. She felt incongruent and inauthentic.

My advice to her: "Go deep inward to find your own voice. Don't try to adopt some voice that you heard or a stereotype of what a colorful voice sounds like."

Fay found her authentic voice, and she later shared, "The voice color part was so illuminating. Now I can feel that my voice is more expressive, yet authentic. It has helped me establish my personal branding."

Three Key Takeaways

- There is no sound more powerful than your speaking voice. It is through your voice that you stir thoughts, evoke emotions, and inspire actions.
- You are your voice. Your voice reflects who you are. When you've developed your voice, you become whole, authentic, and magnetic. Your confidence will soar and your influence will grow.
- Be unapologetically you and let yourself be vulnerable as a woman speaker. It is your feminine energy that sets you apart and inspires people into action.

1   Aung San Su Kyi has been under international criticism since August of 2017 when she kept silent on the violence against Rohingya refugees. This does not change the fact that she is a world-class speaker in her courage to speak up against the brutal military abuses in her country.

2   The world has seen significant decline in people's trust in business, government, NGOs, media, and platforms (e.g. social media) since 2017, according to The Edelman Trust Barometer: *"As we begin 2018, we find the world in a new phase in the loss of trust: the unwillingness to believe information, even from those closest to us."*

3   https://www.poetryfoundation.org/poems/48985/phenomenal-woman

Cynthia Zhai

Cynthia Zhai is a voice coach, speaker, and author. Cynthia has worked with clients from 46 countries across 5 continents, helping professional speakers and senior executives to speak with impact.

Cynthia has been a professional speaker for the past 16 years and her engagements span 15 countries in 4 continents. She has appeared on USA Radio, Radio Singapore's 938Live, Hong Kong Radio 3, and Malaysia Business Radio.

For more on developing a powerful voice:
https://www.powerfulexecutivevoice.com

Connecting: The mindset and psychology of the speech

by Drs. Joyce Carols

Understanding your own mind and the mind and behavior of others is the beginning of crafting a speech that engages, that moves, and that your audience will remember and even put into action.

Most speakers know how to deliver content in a timely, efficient, and from time to time engaging matter. This type of speech usually only touches the audience on an intellectual level. A world-class speaker will deliver a speech that moves the audience on a profound and emotional level, with long-lasting impact.

So, how do you give this kind of speech and where do you start?

The Psychology of a Good Start

The psychology of a good start begins way before you even set foot on the stage. There are three main components that determine if you deliver a good performance, when you look at it from psychological point of view. Here is a formula for you:

$$SC+M+F=R$$
Self-**C**onfidence + **M**otivation + **F**un = **R**esult of your performance

The Psychology Dictionary Online defines self-confidence as "our self-assurance in trusting our abilities, capacities, and judgments; the belief that we can meet the demands of a task." Do you know what you are talking about? Do you feel confident on a stage or in that dress you are wearing? Do you absolutely believe that you have the ability and capability to be on that stage and deliver your speech? Wearing the right clothing and makeup, using a power pose, dealing with your limiting beliefs, knowing your content and your audience, and speaking from the heart (your true you, your *why*) will increase your confidence and the impact of your speech.

Self-confidence is very important in leadership. Some go as far as to say that "without confidence, there is no leadership."[4] The minute you walk on that stage you are given authority. The audience expects you to lead and to act like a leader. Stanley Milgram's controversial experiments[5] in the early 1960s showed that it's very hard for most of us to resist authority. Our brain is simply wired to follow leaders.

G.A. Miller[6] described motivation as all the pushes and prods—biological, social, and psychological—that defeat our laziness and move us to action. To be a good speaker it's important to understand first your motivation for being on stage, and then your audience.

To work this out for yourself, think about your beliefs, the identity you wish to develop, the skills you need to have to develop it, and your absolute *why* (your purpose in life, your reason for being).

Your deepest and strongest motivation to be onstage should come from your purpose as it determines your identity, your beliefs, your capabilities, and your behavior in a certain environment—in this case, the stage. What is your purpose in life and with being a speaker? What drives and really moves you to be on that stage?

The most contagious emotions for your audience are fun and passion. A smile is contagious even for your own brain! Studies have shown that your brain will produce "happy hormones" as soon as you start smiling. So even when you are not happy, keep smiling and you will feel happier after a while. Your audience will feel and mirror your smile and they will start feeling better about you and your speech, too. The flip side of this is the fact that nervousness also is one of the most contagious of emotions. Keep that in mind. A fun and positive mindset will not only make your emotions contagious for your audience, it will also increase your strength, health, and stamina! You will radiate energy and feel stronger and more confident.

You can actively provoke your own positive mindset or state of mind, which will grant you 75 percent more energy than when you have a negative state of mind. You can use a positive trigger list (PTL) to get into the right mindset, even if you're feeling blue, drained, or sad. Your brain does not make a distinction between reality and fiction, so if you bring your brain back to a time in your life when you felt really happy, powerful, or energetic, it will automatically go back to that state and bring your body with it.

So how does a PTL come in handy and work? I always advise my coaching clients to make a PTL on their smartphone. This PTL contains pictures, quotes, and direct links to songs, movies, and events you have loved and that make you feel good, proud, strong, or happy.

Songs, photos, and smells trigger emotions immediately. What's your favorite song? What image makes you smile and feel proud?

My favorite song reminds me of the time I spent in a rehab center trying to learn how to move and walk again after I broke my neck and became paralyzed in an accident in my early twenties. I used to listen to this song when dreaming of fulfilling my childhood dream of playing for the national field hockey team. Even though the neurologist gave me a 99 percent chance of never walking again, I fullheartedly believed I was the 1 percent that would be the exception to the rule. And so I was! Six years later I stood on a field hockey pitch listening to the national anthem as I played, against all odds, in the World Qualifying Series for my national team. This song gives me strength and the belief that anything is possible! If I want to radiate more warmth and love, I'll look at my favorite picture of my two daughters and me and I'll relive that moment. My advice to you is make a PTL of your own and store it in your phone, where you'll have it at hand when you need it most. It can help you to instantly switch your mood.

The Psychology Behind the Colors You Wear

As I said before, the clothes you wear onstage can boost your confidence and energy level. Your favorite colors and the colors you choose to wear say more about you than you know. They not only have a psychological effect on your own behavior, but also on audience perception of who you are.

Blue: Blue is a calm, soothing color that usually reflects wisdom and consistency. You can consider wearing a blue suit, skirt, or blouse when you want to deliver a formal speech with facts and figures (e.g. in a business setting). Blue will evoke feelings of reliability, security, and success for your audience.

Purple: Purple is elegance and lavishness. It is an exceptional color and its rareness in nature highlights its glory. Your audience will perceive a more spiritual and natural energy in your speech.

Green: Green reminds us of the beauty of Mother Nature. Green's calming, fresh effect on the eye and mind gives your audience an open spirit and more access to the right side of their brain. It communicates trustworthiness and harmony.

Red: Red is a symbol of romance and passion worldwide. It is also an outstanding color that captures everyone's attention. Next time you plan on turning heads, simply put on a gorgeous red dress or jacket. You will be perceived as daring, dominant, energetic, and powerful.

Orange: Orange is a combination of cheerfulness and love. The color of fire and heat, orange radiates fun, happiness, warmth, innovation, creativity, emotions, and boldness to your audience.

Yellow: Yellow liberates positive energy, fueling your mind and muscles. Like red, bright yellow always stands out. While yellow can stimulate your own mind and body, your audience will perceive you as caring, warm, optimistic, and positive.

White: White, clean and pure, is the universal color of neutrality. It gives a calm, honest, innocent, peaceful feeling to your audience.

Black: Black is a powerful color to wear. You will be perceived as glamorous, elegant (think of your little black dress), and dignified. However, black can also be seen as safe, tough, and emotionally unavailable. As a woman onstage I would suggest you choose one of the other colors.

The color of your clothes will not only help you get in the right state of mind, it will also subconsciously influence how your audience feels about your speech.

The Psychology Behind Stage Fright

A lot of people are scared of public speaking. In fact, a survey conducted by Newspoll for the training website Reasontospeak.com, to rank our most pervasive fears, showed that in the US, speaking in front of a crowd ranked next to death. So, if you've ever thought that you would rather die than speak in front of an audience, you are not alone.

What's so scary about it? We speak every day, right? We interact and communicate with other people every day. Fortunately, this fear is all in your head. What you need to know is conditioning, and once you master that, you will be sashaying on stages in no time.

Easier said than done? Believe me, I know what fear is. I suffocated on an ER table and saw my own heart monitor go flat when I technically died from a severe allergy attack. My deadly allergy is to a common and frequently used food ingredient. After this near-death experience I had to overcome my fear in order to go on eating in my daily life!

Fear is a chain reaction in the brain that starts with a stressful stimulus and ends with the release of chemicals that cause a racing heart, fast breathing, and energized muscles, among other things, also known as the fight-flight-freeze response. The stimulus could be a spider, a knife at your throat, the sudden thud of your front door, or an auditorium full of people waiting for you to speak.

The brain is a profoundly complex organ. More than 100 billion nerve cells comprise an intricate network of communications that is the starting point of everything we sense, think, and do. Some of these communications lead to conscious thought and action, while others produce autonomic responses. The fear response is almost entirely autonomic: we don't consciously trigger it or even know what's going on until it has run its course.

Because cells in the brain are constantly transferring information and triggering responses, there are dozens of areas of the brain at least peripherally involved in fear. But research has discovered that certain parts of the brain play critical roles in the process:

Parts of the Brain Involved in Fear Response

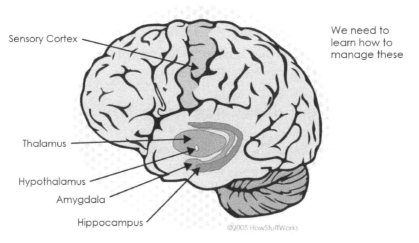

The brain's fear response

- **Thalamus** — decides where to send incoming sensory data from eyes, ears, mouth, and skin)
- **Sensory cortex** — interprets sensory data
- **Hippocampus** — stores and retrieves conscious memories; processes sets of stimuli to establish context
- **Amygdala** — decodes emotions; determines possible threat; stores fear memories
- **Hypothalamus** — activates the fight-freeze-flight response

Although the fear response is usually an autonomic response, we can still learn how to deal with it on a conscious level.

The easiest way to do this is to simply label the perceived emotion in a different way as soon as you feel it. Instead of thinking "Oh no, here we go again, I'm so scared to go on that stage!" you could relabel that same arousal in your energy as, "Yes! I'm so excited to be on that stage!" and smile while you think this.

The fun fact behind relabeling this way is that initially fear shows up in the same area of our brain as excitement does! It's the label we put on it, combined with memories about that same situation, that determine the outcome. Sure, this takes time to practice, but start by relabeling and you'll notice the difference in your bodily response.

The Psychology Behind Connecting with Your Audience

Within a split second after you walk onstage, your audience already starts to create an image, expectations, and emotions about you, before you've even spoken a word! In their mind they subconsciously answer the following two questions: Can I trust this person? Can I respect this person?

Psychologists identify these factors as warmth and competence, and ideally you want to be perceived as having both. The way you walk on (how confident, strong, and determined), will shape the way they'll listen to you. The only time you have at least 100 percent engagement from them is the first 60 seconds after you start to speak. Use these first 60 seconds to trigger their attention, to captivate them by delivering a teaser or ice-breaker (something they did not expect), perhaps in combination with a power movie or sound clip to introduce yourself.

This is your moment to grab the audience, either by using their innate desire to get rid of something they fear or by giving them something they desire. You can keep them engaged on a psychological level by triggering their own emotions, pain, desires, and fears in your speech.

Make it about them and not about you. What are their needs? What do you think is their fear or desire? Can they relate to you and the things you say? Build a bond and common ground first. Do they feel true and honest emotions coming from you? Do you speak with purpose from your heart, from your *why* or your true identity? If you're only speaking out of your mental center and not from your heart, your audience will notice and will connect less easily to what you have to say.

A big difference between male and female audiences is the way they listen to stories. Men have a tendency to want to fix things and come up with a solution. So, give them a more mental, rational solution. Women, however, want to ease your pain, care for you, let you tell your story, and sympathize with you, so give them a bonding solution so that they can share your emotions. For mixed audiences it's crucial to keep this in mind and deliver a mix of both kinds of solutions in order for them to connect with your message.

Real connection with your audience on a psychological level also has to do with your verbal and non-verbal communication.

Let's start with your **verbal communication**. Although you might be shocked to learn that your verbal communication (the words you say) is only seven percent of your overall communication, the impact words have on the body are huge. In the 1980s the Japanese scientist Masaru Emoto did profound research on the effect that spoken words had on water, and his findings were stunning. Water crystals would completely deform when exposed to a class of schoolkids repeating a curse word. The same water in another glass was exposed to the same group of children, but to this water they said only nice words. The water crystals in the second glass remained beautifully shaped and formed. When you consider that our bodies consist of about 60–70 percent water, you'll immediately understand the impact negative words can have on how your audience will feel.

You can also trigger memories, feelings, and emotions in your audience by coloring your sentences. For example, let's say I want to tell you about how I heard the news, in my early twenties, that I would never walk again. I could just tell you that the neurologist told me so, or I could tell you, "When I opened my eyes, through the bandage and the neck collar that supported my broken bones, I found myself lying flat on a hard iron table. I could see only white jackets around me and I heard people scream, run, and shout orders on how to keep the patient alive, how to keep her neck stable, and what to do next. It took a while for me to realize I was in a hospital and that the person they were talking about was me! I was paralyzed and I would never walk again! With great fear I saw a stern-looking doctor approach me and with a hard, dark voice he bluntly told me that I had broken my neck and that I would spend the rest of my life in a wheelchair!"

The listener's brain is wired to form recognizable images from the information you provide. The more you color your words and the more recognizable details you give, the greater the impact of your words will be. The less you color your delivery, the more listeners will color it with their own paradigm, and if your words do not match their paradigm and recognizable pictures in their brain, you will lose your audience's attention.

Strong, positive words will emphasize your statements, and so will **silence**. A pause of three seconds will put emphasis on what you just said before it. This will give the audience time to process the information you've given them, and it will keep them in suspense for what's coming next.

When considering your **non-verbal communication**, please make sure that your body supports your words. With vocal pitch you can emphasize or de-emphasize your words. The lower your voice is, the more your speech will be perceived as credible by your audience. By controlling loud and soft tones, you can indicate importance, capture the audience through shock effect, and really emphasize your emotions, feelings, or meaning. As a woman, you have a natural speaking voice that is higher than that of the average man. Keep this in mind and try to practice lowering it from time to time.

Arm gestures can also support what you have to say; however, remember to reverse your gestures, as in a mirror image, for your audience. What does this mean, when put into practice? Our brain is wired to think of progress, growth, and the future as a line that goes from bottom left to top right, or simply as a gesture from left to right. When saying that your audience could grow by using your techniques, if you gesture with your right arm up, they will not believe you! Why? Because your right side is their left side and their brain sees an arm go towards the past! So, if you want to indicate growth, use your left arm and point left side up. If you want to talk about the past or going back, use your right arm.

Audience		
future	now	past

Adapt your arm and hand movements
to the audience's perspective

The brain interprets space as time – use arm
movements to help your audience

Once you take a close look at the way the brain interprets space as time, it will not surprise you to learn that every stage angle also has significance for your audience. Moving towards the left side of the stage will tell your audience you are showing them the future. If you walk towards the right side of your stage, their brain will automatically take them back in time. Please note that the left and right brain game as described above counts only for audiences in countries that read and write from left to right!

A strong power pose will help your audience see you as the leader you are expected to be on that stage and will give your brain signals to distribute more "strength and power" hormones into your system. A typical power pose is head up, with feet firmly on the ground and back straight, then smile and look into the room.

The Psychology of a Good Ending

A recent Microsoft study shows that due to the extensive use of smartphones, the time the average person can give full attention to something has been reduced to only eight seconds! Key statements and repeating your message are essential to what your audience will remember of your speech. The good news is that if we hear the same thing a few times, our brain will start to believe it's the truth. You can use this knowledge of the "illusory truth effect," as we call it in psychological terms, to your advantage by repeating your key message. Determine and write down the key statements (no more than three) you want your audience to remember. Make sure to come back to them at least three times—at the beginning, middle, and end of your speech.

End your speech with either a summary or repetition of your opening. This will close the story loop in your listeners' brains and give them room to process what you've said. An open end will leave their brains confused, which may cause negative feelings of unmet expectation, frustration, or disappointment about your speech.

As I said at the opening of this chapter, the psychology and mindset of speech is all about understanding the mind and behavior of others. Use the knowledge I've shared with you in this chapter (combined with the rest of the fabulous advice in this book) to your advantage and I'm sure you'll rock every stage on earth!

> **Three Key Takeaways**
>
> - Always make sure your own mind is in its best state before you enter the stage.
> - Your listeners' brains will subconsciously determine whether or not they believe you, feel you, or can engage with your speech.
> - Repetition of your key statement(s) is key to your success.

And because you've been dying to know since the beginning of this chapter, my song, the one that helped me thrive: "I Will Survive," by Gloria Ganor.

---

1   Francisco Dao, "Without Confidence, There is No Leadership," January 27, 2008, INC Online. https://www.inc.com/leadership-blog/2008/01/without_confidence_there_is_no.html

2   https://en.wikipedia.org/wiki/Milgram_experiment

3   G.A. Miller, *Psychology: The Science of Mental Life*, Harper and Row, 1962. Referred to in Richard Gross, *Psychology: The Science of Mind and Behaviour 7th Edition*, Hodder Education, 2015.

Joyce Carols

Drs. Joyce Carols is the Founder of Enjoy EsC, an executive training and coaching company focusing on mindset and behavior for high-performance women. Her mission is to empower female leaders to do, achieve, or overcome anything and to enjoy every minute of their lives.

Her Drs. degree in psychology and psycho-social sciences, along with over two decades of experience and her own journey of overcoming adversity, ground her in both science and the real-world challenges of high achievement.

She's a proud foster mom of two beautiful girls and a TEDx speaker, and she represented the Netherlands internationally in both field hockey and acro-diving. She has worked for well-known Fortune 500 Companies globally.

For more on professional success and personal energy:
www.JoyceCarols.com

Shared Stories Stick

by Anjali Sharma

History is Shared Stories. If we don't tell ours, how will our daughters learn?

At 4:00 am the alarm rings. I'm taking the early flight to Kuala Lumpur to give a keynote. I'm leaving the morning of the talk. This way, I get to spend more time with my daughter.

I'm a bit unsettled. I mentally check the schedule I've arranged for her day: school drop-off, pick-up, play-date, and meals. All covered! Now my thoughts can turn to the keynote. Am I prepared? Am I organized?

But in Kuala Lumpur, long immigration queues, and horrendous traffic, banish the subtleties of my talk from my mind! I'm now wondering if I will make it in time.

I reach the venue in time. The stage manager says: "You are wearing a dress. Where are we going to hook the mike?" I handle it. I've done this before.

But we aren't finished. My earrings interfere with this mic. I take them off and feel less composed. Then, just five minutes into my talk, the heel of one shoe breaks. Could anything else test me today? I am overwhelmed. I really want to cry!

That was then. I had no idea that experience would become a staple story. I've told it often in my engagements, and years later people still ask me about it.

Sheryl Sandberg made a last-minute addition of a story to her TED Talk, "Why We Have Too Few Women Leaders." The story was about her daughter clinging to her legs and telling her not to leave home.

Sandberg admitted her initial reaction when a friend suggested that she tells that story was, "Are you kidding? I'm going to get on a stage and admit my daughter was clinging to my leg?"

However, this story was an integral part of the talk that helped to launch the Lean In movement, sparking group meetings and events worldwide, as well as educational and corporate partnerships. Shared stories stick.

But how shall we tell them? More importantly, which ones do we, as women, need to tell?

This chapter offers answers to some of these questions.

Story Connections

Rarely can a response make something better—what makes something better is a connection. —Dr. Brené Brown

Recently, a client (let's call her Maria) asked for help with a talk on women in leadership. She's well equipped to speak on this topic. It's one she's passionate about.

She researched thoroughly to produce her first draft. It included every aspect she wanted to touch on but lacked oomph.

Why was she invited to give this talk? Not to do research, but because she is passionate about the subject. Where was the passion in this draft?

Carmine Gallo highlights entrepreneurial passion in his book, *Talk Like TED*. Entrepreneurial passion is what you experience when you hear something profoundly meaningful. I suggest to Maria: "Say something personal." Her response? "I don't want to talk about myself. Can't we focus on the topic?"

It's a common reaction. She thinks that talking about personal achievements may not work. Unfortunately, she's damn right! A Harvard study shows Maria's fear is well-founded... for women! Success and likeability correlate positively for men, but negatively for women.[7]

Researchers asked respondents to read a case based on a successful, female Silicon Valley venture capitalist, Heidi Roize. Half the students read a story about "Heidi" and the other half a story about "Howard."

Both male and female respondents ranked the characters' competence equally. After all, their accomplishments were identical. But when it came to how appealing they might be as a colleague, Howard was rated as appealing, and Heidi as selfish, "not the type of person you'd want to hire or work for."

So, Maria was right to be wary of sharing personal success stories. I suggested she describe an incident that would create a human connection without triggering a negative response. She agreed, reluctantly. Here's the result, which became the start of her talk.

"After years as a leader in companies on several continents, you'd think I'd be an expert on women in leadership. But the truth is, I am not.

Some years ago, my husband, teenage daughter, and I made a really, really tough decision. We sent our daughter overseas to study. We all agreed it was best for her future. What made it so hard was that, if I wanted to continue my career, I couldn't join her.

Separating from your daughter isn't easy. Any mother in the room knows this. At the airport, we said goodbye. She and I were acting bravely and we both thought we were pretty cool about the situation. But as my eyes followed her through the glass of the departure hall, tears rolled down my face. She turned. I saw she was crying, too. But what were our choices? Join her and finish my career? Or keep her at home, and spoil hers—before it began? Women in Leadership can be a deeply personal and testing choice."

With this story, Maria connected to her audience.

She sent me a text: "I have been asked to join other women on leadership boards. And my talk was celebrated!" This sounds spontaneous—but only if you don't know the insight that helped her choose that story and tell it just the way it should be told.

This is how you can avoid the "bragging trap" that awaits women speakers in particular.

Choosing and Assembling the Story

When you are choosing and assembling your story, here are four insights that can help.

Resonance is required: Both Sandberg and Maria chose stories that connect to a problem felt by women in leadership: the balancing act of work and life. Both stories make the audience feel like it could be their own story. If your story doesn't resonate with the audience, then it's not *true* for them.

Emotion is essential: Both Sandberg's and Maria's stories admit the moments they illustrated were difficult. Did you notice the use of words like hard, crying, etc.? Descriptions, not display, of emotions is essential to make the audience feel the story.

Events, not examples: It would have been easy for both Sandberg and Maria to simply say, "I am representative of working women who have children and find it hard to achieve a work-life balance." However, that would not have engaged the audience at all. Engagement comes via the events that made their stories compelling. The events in Maria's case included going to the airport and seeing her daughter across the departure hall. By narrating the events, you invite the listener to be a part of the story. They don't just listen to you, they go to the airport with you!

Personal is preferred: All three stories we've discussed in this chapter are personal. They are the best stories to tell because when they are your personal experiences, you deliver them authentically.

If you use these insights in choosing and assembling a story, you will connect with the audience instantly without risking being labelled a bragger.

Fighting Failures with Stories

As Judge Victoria Pratt likes to say, failure is just an event, not a characteristic. Women can't *be* failures.

Eve is head of communications for a multinational organization. She called me for help in preparing a talk on trade law changes and their impact in her industry.

I asked, "Where do you want my help? Content? Delivery? Something else?"

Her response: "None of those. I have anxiety about this talk."

Anxiety? Isn't that a medical problem? I suggested we meet and talk. I asked, "What is causing the anxiety?"

She seemed uncomfortable. Then, with a sigh, she tells me: "Recently I presented to some senior business leaders, including my immediate boss. I knew some people in the audience don't like me. After only a few minutes, I froze. I forgot what I came to say. I saw myself as a fraud and I felt that those who worried me had achieved their desired outcome. A couple of days later there was a rumor that I'm not on my A-game. I was very embarrassed. I now fear the stage."

Her tears flowed. I frantically looked for some tissues.

Sadly, one failure and a rumor had defined Eve in her own mind. Transient failures can be fodder for a woman's no-permission-to-fail mindset.

A study by HP showed that men happily apply for a job even if they meet only 60 percent of the qualifications. Women tend to hold back unless they meet 100 percent.[8] They don't allow themselves to fail.

I think one reason may be girls not playing informal sports during their formative years. Boys are into sports before girls, and I don't mean formal sports—I mean play that happens at home in everyday life. They learn early on how to win, how to lose, and to be OK with either. Women don't have the same preparation and are less comfortable with potential failure.

I had to help Eve rise above this possibility. There is nothing that guarantees that you will always get applause! But there is something that guarantees that you can rise above failure if it occurs, and I'm going to tell you how to do that.

I asked Eve to acknowledge the rumor and tell a story that contradicts the rumor with a bit of satire. This is the result:

"What happened two weeks ago made everyone including me feel that my talks don't really lead to the desired outcomes. Trust me, I have felt that way. So, I went up to my boss and suggested that maybe someone else should talk today and I was expecting her to say, 'Yes, I agree.' Instead, she walked up to the whiteboard and started scribbling all the talks I have been part of and showed me that one failed talk can't be my personal lack of ability. I want to thank Vivian (my boss) for her faith in me, and with that, I will begin my presentation for today."

By acknowledging the rumor and telling a story that contradicts it, Eve made a wise and strategic move. You too can go beyond the failures. Do not let them define you. Use the power of a story to be a perfect antidote to a rumor about you or your topic.

Three Key Takeaways

- This chapter aims to empower women to use storytelling in those moments we feel overwhelmed by pressures that are unique to us.
- We use stories not just because they might lead to an innovation, for example a mic that can fit on a dress, but because if generations before us had shared their stories we would not be in the position we are. This time, we owe it to our daughters.
- Use stories fortified with insights and strategies to create a connection, fight the failure, and see yourself succeed.

And in closing, to paraphrase from Elena Favilli's *Good Night Stories for Rebel Girls:*

To the women of the world.
Aim higher. Fight harder.
When in doubt, tell a story.
We owe this to our daughters.[9]

---

1   https://www.leadershippsychologyinstitute.com/women-the-leadership
    -labyrinth-howard-vs-heidi/
2   https://www.forbes.com/sites/womensmedia/2014/04/28/act-now-to-shrink
    -the-confidence-gap/#2f3f2f205c41
3   Elena Favilli, *Good Night Stories for Rebel Girls: 100 Tales of Extraordinary
    Women,* Timbuktu Labs, Inc., 2016

Anjali Sharma

Anjali Sharma is one of the leading business storytelling consultants in Asia Pacific. She helps business leaders, data analysts, sales professionals, and TEDx speakers find and tell stories. Anjali has worked in corporate roles for over 18 years in Australia, Singapore, and India.

Her background constantly informs her work, giving her an approach that is not just theoretical but based on extensive experience, knowledge, and understanding of strategic issues for companies as well as issues that employees face in delivering their best work.

Anjali partners with Global 1000 companies including Shell, SAP, Microsoft, and Danone.

For more on storytelling:
https://narrative.com.sg/what-we-offer/narrative-speaks/

PART 2

WHAT COMES BEFORE THE TALK

Finding your niche, building
the virtual stage, building your
name and your authenticity

A Corporate Speaking Journey

by Siân Brown

A rabbit caught in headlights is the only way to describe my early experience of public speaking. In one of my university courses we had to deliver a monthly presentation to our fellow students in a lecture theatre—the worst module ever, in my mind! I would sweat profusely, to the point where I had to wear cotton pads under my arms to try to stop the embarrassment. I felt awkward and imagined the effect of my monotone voice being similar to a that of a tape of music to fall asleep to. I somehow got through the course and swore I would never get up to speak in front of a crowd again.

When I started working in the banking industry it was easy to avoid such torture. That is, until I was several years into my career and started really looking at leaders I admired, what made them different, and how could I get to that next level. What was obvious from observing them was that they had a common trait—they were great public speakers. They could hold a crowd's attention, deliver messages with authenticity, and handle the unexpected. I begrudgingly realized that if I was going to grow into the next, more improved version of me, I had to face my fear and get out there in front of an audience.

I started small, by forming a network group which I hosted on a quarterly basis, forcing myself to get up on stage and discuss topics and interview experts. Each time I had to face my worst fears and be front and center. I still sweated and shook, and had to force myself to get up, although I could take pride in myself in that I was at least giving it a shot. My turning point was going on a leadership development course that covered, along with many other modules in its extensive scope, voice training techniques, improvisation, and delivering with presence. These sessions gave me some invaluable techniques which I use to this day, helping me manage my fear of getting onstage and being heard.

The voice training session taught me basic principles of "waking" my voice up before important sessions, whether for a meeting with three people or to present to a room of a few hundred. It made me realize that I could train my voice to sound louder and more confident, which would help with landing the impact of the message. I faced the hard reality that I had tried to hide my voice over the years, due to schoolyard taunts as a child: when I moved from the Medway towns in Kent to a private school in Wales, I was teased relentlessly for my "common" accent. Like all kids I was a true chameleon, and a few years later I had subconsciously rounded out my accent and I was no longer teased. The joy of fitting in was short-lived, however. When I moved from the private school to a normal comprehensive school, I was seen as a posh kid, teased for my plummy accent, and pushed about the playground. Once again I changed my accent, and the result was a non-descript, boring, chameleon accent—and an underlying fear of being teased about how I sounded.

By identifying, and then accepting, the reason I didn't want my voice to be heard, I was able to move on. The voice training was practical, and I entertained my children for many mornings by warming up my voice as an opera singer would, teaching them how they could throw their own voices further across the room without shouting. To this day I use the tips I learned then, whether it be sitting straight with both feet on the ground to open the diaphragm up to its maximum (works very well in meetings and on the phone) or ensuring that I've loosened my vocal chords when I'm getting ready for a big event.

I initially came to the training on improvisation with a hefty amount of skepticism. What was a group of comedians going to teach me that would help me be a better leader? As it turned out, quite a lot. They made me realize that my anxiety could be reduced by focusing less on me and my feelings and focusing more on everyone else in the room. Truly listening to the room and emotionally connecting to what people were feeling, not just looking at content, took my own inner critic's eye away from myself. It also became much easier for me to work with the audience, adapting to whatever situation arose, because I was far more present with the people and how they were responding. My crude summary of the nuts and bolts of the improvisation training, if you're not already a convert, is that it is about the positive reception of any question or statement (in other words, respond with a *yes, and...*) in addition to sharpening your listening skills.

The last of the training modules had the most impact for me: Delivering with Presence. There were so many takeaways from this that I was just sorry not to have done it ten years earlier! This module taught me everything from how to condense any speech onto one sheet of A4 paper to the dreaded video practice routine. Condensing to one page has become one of my favorite strategies for any prep item. I have used it extensively for public speaking, and it's also my go-to tool when I'm preparing for the five-minute slot with the visiting C-suite leader or shaping how a controls workshop will be run for a day.

And the dreaded video practice—I love this. It works, it's impactful, and it gives your kids a laugh. I video myself delivering a key speech or message and I keep re-doing until I can actually watch the video without wanting to vomit or laugh hysterically.

The replay helps you pick up on so much—your tone, filler words, parts of the speech you're not comfortable with due to lack of deep knowledge or detailed information (which gives you the chance to find that information), how relaxed your body language is, and areas where you're too fast or too slow.

And not only all of that, but the fact that you are practicing out loud gives your jaw muscles a workout on what will become a standard routine, after two or three practices. This means what you have to say becomes captured as part of your muscle memory, leaving more space in your brain to be thinking about how you're delivering and what else is happening in the room. Rehearsing for a speaker session on conduct in financial services while my two sons pull faces and do everything they could think of to distract me set me up well for an audience of compliance officers from across the industry.

The last two nuggets of wisdom I took from the course on delivering with presence were to believe in your topic in order to be authentic and to practice, practice, practice. Well-armed, I set about using the tools and techniques I'd been taught to see if I could become the leader I envisioned.

I had the fortune during this time to be introduced to a toastmasters society though a mentee of mine. To my surprise, he asked me to speak at a toastmasters panel event on communication skills, with the only caveat being that I had to be prepared for honest feedback from the audience, not only on my content but also on how I delivered it. Being self-aware of my fear, I figured that getting up in front of a professional public speaking network would have a kill-or-cure effect on my ambitions.

The panel went brilliantly; feedback on content was great and I waited as nervously as a talent show contestant for the evaluator feedback, which included the *Ah* Counter's report—yes, an official role in a toastmasters society is to count filler words, such as *um, ah,* and *well,* used by the speaker.

Others on the panel received fair, constructive comments regarding their *um*ing and *ah*ing and feedback on impact of delivery. My turn came, and I received the best feedback I could have hoped for. My delivery style was authentic, engaging, humorous at the right moments, and inclusive of the audience and the other panel members.

Why was I so shocked it had gone so well? I realized that I had been my absolute worse inner critic, and that this was the first time in my career I had actually received such honest, constructive feedback on one of the areas that was causing me such paralysis. By being more present with the room, by being able to add the *yes, and…* element to the debate, and by being incredibly passionate on the topic, I had nailed it.

Even the *Ah* Counter was complimentary, identifying just a few *so* fillers (and the great thing is, now I know that's my filler weakness and I am more conscious about not using it).

I meant this chapter to be about public speaking and my corporate career. How, then, does it all link together? I began doing a fair amount of external public speaking when I joined the board of the British Chamber of Commerce in Singapore and chaired the Women in Business group. My joining the board coincided with the leadership course, which meant I had real public platforms in which to practice my new toolkit and to grow my own confidence.

What I quickly realized was that the tools I was using for the public speaking events could, and should, be used to help me succeed in many of the internal meeting situations in which I found myself. The basics skills and competences that you grow with public speaking are ones you need in every situation within the corporate environment. For example, when delivering a pitch for a new project—how I deliver the message, my assurance over owning and believing in the project's benefit, my clarity in communicating the ask, and my ability to read the room to see where I may need to improvise on the direction I take the conversation are all areas where I can draw on the tools I've been developing for public speaking.

Three Key Takeaways

Has the experience I've developed in public speaking helped me in my corporate journey? Absolutely. It has helped validate to me that my inner critic was holding me back and needed to be put to bed. It's also helped me pay it forward to my colleagues and teams by being able to share with them the tools or experiences I've gained. I'd recommend anyone that fears public speaking or who wants to be heard more in the corporate environment to do the following:

- Identify what's holding you back/underlying your fear. Accept it, address it, and move on.
- Get the right toolkit: tips/techniques/training, feedback, and practice, practice, practice.
- Learn to improvise. This will help you connect with your audience and ensure that you can adapt to anything you encounter as a speaker.

I am far from the end of my own development journey and I do not always follow the advice I've laid out. However, each time I don't follow my own pearls of wisdom I kick myself, for I didn't deliver to the best that I now know I have in me.

Siân Brown

Siân Brown has worked in the financial services industry for over 20 years, spending the earlier part of her career in the UK, Europe, and US and the latter years in Japan, Hong Kong, and Singapore. Her career has been driven by seeking out opportunities to provide platforms for continuous learning. As a passionate advocate for diversity and inclusion, Siân moderates and speaks at many events to support action for parity. In contributing to this book, Siân hopes to encourage other women to embrace their fears and become awesome public speakers, ultimately helping them achieve their ambitions.

Standing Out: Leveraging niche markets to become an expert

by Marian Bacol-Uba

Speaking professionally is very rewarding. You have the ability to make an impact on thousands, even millions of people with your message. There is definitely room in the marketplace for more speakers, especially women speakers. There is a demand for more diversity on stages, so this is a great time to take advantage of the opportunity.

You may have heard of the "Ten Thousand Hours Rule." This idea comes from the work of psychologist K. Anders Ericsson and was popularized by best-selling author Malcolm Gladwell in his book *Outliers*. He wrote that "ten thousand hours is the magic number of greatness."[10]

Although continuous practice helps to hone your speaking skills, you do not need to be on a stage for ten thousand hours in order to be an expert. One of the fastest and most effective ways to stand out as a speaker is to find your niche market.

A niche market is as a smaller, focused group of a larger demographic, with its own particular needs or preferences.

Why is This Valuable to Know?

Once you have identified your niche, you can leverage it to become a well-known expert and grow your influence in that group. This is how you build authority and credibility. Authority and credibility are not something you can buy or achieve overnight. They must be cultivated and that takes time. However, cultivating them in your niche market speeds up the process.

Like most people who are just beginning their speaking careers, I thought that choosing a niche market would pigeonhole me. I thought casting a wide net would give me more opportunities. I feared that focusing on a niche market topic would be limiting. Actually, the opposite is true. Catering to a niche market allowed me to go deep with my audience and message as well as create targeted marketing materials that increased speaking opportunities.

Even though you may have many topics you would like to speak on, you must learn to focus your topic.

Do not try to be everything for everyone. Remember, a jack-of-all-trades is the master of none. You want your audience to know you as the expert for something specific so when opportunities within that niche market arise, you are their go-to industry authority figure. You want to make your name synonymous with your niche topic.

If you are reading this book, speaking is something you are passionate about and you want to make a positive impact in the world. The world needs and wants to hear your message! No one else can match your exact story, expertise, and authentic voice. We need more women of all backgrounds and experiences to step up and stand out! That being said, how is your audience going to find you when your efforts are spread out all over the place?

In this chapter I will share exact steps and key insights on how I have identified a niche market that I am passionate about with an audience that I serve daily. The more I cultivate my niche market, the more my influence grows. When you position yourself as an expert, opportunities for speaking and other collaborations will present itself to you. Remember that you are not only a speaker, but also a brand. There are many other avenues than just on stage to sharing your message of impact to the world. You can also reach your audience and speak through videos, podcasts, television, and various social media channels.

How do I Find My Niche Market?

1. **Identify your interests and passions**

If you plan to make a long speech, make sure you actually like what you are speaking about. If you don't care about the topic, you may lose interest in it quickly. Your audience will also be able to sense if you are truly passionate about that topic or just lukewarm about it. When you are not entirely enthusiastic about the topic, you may not be able to find the inner drive to persevere through challenges and roadblocks as you grow your speaking career.

Identify your interests and passions by asking questions like these:

> *What do I spend a lot of my time and money on?*
>
> *What do I look forward to doing?*
>
> *What topics do I like to continuously learn about?*
>
> *What clubs or organizations do I belong to?*
>
> *What kind of books, magazines, and online publications do I like to read?*

Create a list of your interests and passions from your answers to those questions. Then narrow down those topics to more specific subsets of each topic. It is better to be specific rather than broad.

When I did this exercise, "health and wellness" was on my list. However, that is still a very broad topic. I distilled it down further to "holistic health and wellness." From there I was able to refine the niche further to the specific practice of meditation. I meditate daily and am truly passionate about it. It has changed my life and it is something I want to share with others. I regularly speak and teach workshops on meditation and mindfulness. I love sharing this ancient practice with my audience and giving them the tools to incorporate it into their modern, daily lives. I have given talks such as "Meditation for Creatives and Sparking Creativity" (for creatives and designers), "Meditation and Mindfulness for Modern Women" (for a professional women's organization), "Timeline Healing: Meditation for Trauma Survivors" (for sexual abuse survivors), "Money, Mental Health, and Meditation" (for finance professionals), and many more.

2. Speak about your personal experiences

Another way to find your niche market topic is by sharing your personal experiences. Audiences connect with you on a deeper level when you speak authentically and from a place of vulnerability. Dr. Brené Brown is a research professor at the University of Houston Graduate College of Social Work, a *New York Times* bestselling author, and a keynote speaker. Her 2010 Houston TEDx Talk, "The Power of Vulnerability," is one of the top ten most viewed TED Talks in the world. By sharing her personal story of failures, challenges, and struggles in this TED Talk and beyond, Dr. Brown has positioned herself as the expert in tapping into your vulnerability for success in life, love, career, and more.

Perhaps you overcame a specific sickness, such as breast cancer, or you healed an eating disorder through adopting a plant-based diet. Maybe you want to talk about cultivating leadership in corporate environments through emotional intelligence. One of my signature talks is "Survivor to Thriver," in which I share my inspiring journey as a survivor of childhood sexual abuse, substance abuse, and suicide. I weave in my personal stories with my niche market expertise in meditation and holistic health and wellness.

Create a list of potential niche markets based on your answers identifying your interests and passions and on your personal experiences. Once you have your list of potential niche markets, rank the list from your least to most favorite focus topics. Now that you have narrowed it down to three or four niche market topics, it is time to do your research. Are there other speakers and experts who talk about this particular topic? Are there events and conferences around this niche market? What are they? What is your unique approach and story for this niche market? Knowing the audience and key players of your niche market makes it easier to come up with a strategic plan to build your authority and credibility within this demographic.

How do I Build Authority and Influence in My Niche Market?

1. **Collaboration over competition**

Working together with other women speakers can accelerate your speaking career. Instead of viewing other women as your competition, see them as your allies. As a collaborative group, we can combine resources, referrals, and knowledge. Not all women speakers will be speaking about the same topic as you, even if it's in the same niche. For example, a conference around veganism can have multiple speakers talking about food, activism, health, fashion, beauty, and more. Most conferences and events have multiple tracks and breakout sessions that require various speakers. I've had many referrals come through other women. I was invited to speak at an online summit for conscious and mindful female entrepreneurs because a fellow woman speaker, with whom I connected in a Facebook group, referred me to the summit organizer.

Speaking opportunities are not limited to existing conferences and events. Another way to collaborate is to create your own events. You can start by organizing small local events or meetups. As your audience grows, your events will grow as well. You can invite other women to speak on their expert topics at your event. Organizing a panel discussion is another great way to bring several women speakers together to share their expertise. For example, I organized a panel discussion about mental health and entrepreneurship. I focused on meditation and mental health, while the three other speakers talked about their own expertise as it related to the event topics.

2. Capitalize on social media and build your brand

Millions of people are on their mobile phones and computers all day and spend a lot of time on social media channels such as Instagram, YouTube, Twitter, and Facebook. Make sure your website and bios for all your social media channels are professional and consistent across all platforms. Talk about your niche topic often and give value to your audience. Create educational and informative content that positions you as an expert. Answer questions, engage with your audience, and interact and connect with other experts, event organizers, and meeting planners in your niche market.

I attended a wellness retreat in Tulum, Mexico and one of the retreat organizers was a watercolor artist who had established herself as an expert in her niche market. She taught online classes on watercolor painting, made videos on that topic, displayed her artwork on Instagram, and built her brand through social media. She told me that many of her speaking opportunities about building a lucrative business as a watercolor artist came from people who saw her videos, tutorials, and artwork through YouTube and Instagram. She has been invited to lead watercolor workshops all over the world, from New York to Florence, Italy.

3. Find the decision-makers in your niche market

When you have identified your niche market, you can really home in on finding the top decision-makers who select speakers. Find out where those decision-makers hang out, what organizations and associations they belong to, and what events they attend. Once you know that information, you can become involved in those same organizations and attend the same events so that you can network with those decision-makers. Build organic relationships and provide them value. Show them that you are an expert in that niche market so that you are top-of-mind when it is time to book speakers for their upcoming events.

4. Contribute to niche publications and podcasts

Many public speakers build their credibility and expert status by writing for niche online publications and magazines and being interviewed on podcasts. People perceive that if you have written a published article or been interviewed on a podcast, especially a high-ranking one, you are a person of authority on your topic. Most publications allow you to add a short bio and links. Podcast guests are often given the opportunity to talk about their businesses and provide their contact info. Publications and podcasts are always looking for fresh content so there are endless opportunities available. You just need to do your research, pitch yourself well, submit professional articles, and be an engaging and impactful podcast guest who delivers massive value to the podcast host and their audience.

There are many routes to a successful speaking career. However, by following these steps and focusing on a niche market and topic, your credibility will be established much faster.

By accelerating your path to becoming a successful public speaker, you will be able to get your message out more effectively to inspire and empower more people. We need women like you to stand out and speak up!

Three Key Takeaways

- Becoming an expert in your niche market will increase your influence faster in a shorter amount of time.
- Collaborating with other women speakers and professionals creates more impact, opportunities and success.
- Establish credibility and authority through various social media channels and media platforms.

---

1   Malcolm Gladwell, *Outliers,* Little, Brown, and Co., 2008.

Marian Bacol-Uba

Marian Bacol-Uba is a TEDx Speaker, Conscious Business Coach and the Founder of Thriver Lifestyle. She is also a Certified Pranayama and Meditation Teacher and the host of Thriver Lifestyle Podcast and Mondays with Marian on YouTube. Marian helps women step into their POWER and soulfully THRIVE in life and business.

In addition to online coaching and group programs, Marian speaks about conscious entrepreneurship, leadership, women's empowerment and wellness. She merges her 15+ years of marketing, event production and business development experience with her mission to create positive social impact and help elevate the collective consciousness. Marian has been featured on CBS Los Angeles, Thrive Global, Elephant Journal, Bustle, SWAAY Media and over 35 podcasts and publications.

For more on thriving and empowerment: www.marianbacoluba.com. Follow Marian on Instagram @mbacoluba.

Own Your Digital Stage First

by Andrea T. Edwards, The Digital Conversationalist

If you have a strong desire to be onstage (which I presume you do if you're reading this book), the best way to secure your place and future as a speaker is to own your place on the digital stage *first*. However, whether you want to excel on a physical stage or digital platforms, nothing short of world-class cuts it.

Executives and businesses that hire and sponsor professional speakers today understand that social media leadership is a critical role for future advancement for themselves and their employees. They are starting to recognize that in order to advance, having social leadership skills is a must. The pendulum has swung towards social leadership, at the executive level, but the confusion continues about how to do it brilliantly.

However, even while business leaders have accepted social media leadership as a critical skill and appreciate that it's a challenging *new muscle* to build, they often tell me that what they see on social media today does not match *their* idea of what world-class looks like.

These leaders express disappointment at seeing professionals share information that delivers no value to an audience. They are put off by self-promotion and narcissistic behavior. And they are frustrated, really frustrated, because they know social media should be a better place for engagement and thought leadership. If you are showing up on social media and it's all about you, delivers no value to your audience, or is not well thought-out for your audience, expect this to turn off the very business leaders you hope to influence.

To succeed as a professional speaker and establish yourself as a leader in your field, building credibility and respect on a digital level with this executive audience should be one of your biggest priorities. This is how you firmly put your stake in the ground as *the* expert who can't be ignored. This is how you build a tribe of raving fans. This is how you are recommended as the go-to professional in your field. And this is how you start a professional speaking career today.

Start with building a powerful presence on the digital stage and your step towards the physical stage will naturally follow. Become known for what you want to speak about long before you step under the bright lights on the stage.

Social leadership is a great gift for anyone wanting to break into the lucrative business of professional speaking. It opens the door to so many possibilities. But it requires focus, commitment, and execution at a level of excellence that ensures you cannot be ignored.

What's Your Focus?

The starting point for building a powerful digital presence is to define your focus. As speakers we are fortunate to know this already, because it is our driving force for wanting to be onstage in the first place. We are already committed to and passionate about the message we want to share!

Focus is everything when succeeding on the digital stage. I recommend that at least 80 percent of what you do on your professional digital profiles be to share insights on your focus area, every day. Become a consistent, powerful voice in your field of expertise. Become the one-stop shop for knowledge in your area, the person who shares the best on the topic you want to be known for. Build the trust of your audience by being the digital superstar in your field.

Defining your focus is the starting point of social leadership, and whether or not you find this easy to do, it's not the end of the journey. Once you find that place to start and get going, the exercise of being a social leader forces you to continue going deeper.

Most people who know me would consider my voice to be strong both digitally *and* physically, and yet I don't believe I've gotten to the depths of where I will eventually go in defining my own voice. I'm getting closer, but it's a journey I joined a quarter of the way through my life—bringing all of that life and professional experience with me—and now, nearly halfway through, I have to keep digging deeper and deeper into my conscious and subconscious to find the message I really want to share. Start your own journey with focus, but appreciate that it will evolve, too.

Why Do You Do What You Do?

Tying your presence to a powerful *why* is also a critical part of succeeding. If you can tie your heart and mind to your *why*, it is even more powerful. It's your reason for being there in the first place.

My *why*? I want to change the world by helping everyone understand the power we all have to own our voice on social media and to make a positive impact in the world. For a long time I lost my belief that I could change the world, but today, with social media, we all have a voice and the ability to impact millions with our positive message.

Likewise, social leadership as a culture within business changes how we do business and changes how business is done. It empowers employees, forcing them to be externally focused, and it breaks down silos and hierarchies. It transforms business for the future of work, where everyone lives and works *out loud*, and I believe a social leadership culture is the tool of disruption for our time.

My *why* is tied to helping all people understand the power and responsibility that comes with social leadership and to helping transform how business is done—whatever the business. The power of my *why* is that it gives me the motivation and inspiration to show up every day on social channels because it is tied to something much bigger than myself.

What is your *why*? Why do you do what you do? If you can answer this, you will be beyond powerful.

Self-confidence is a Barrier to Entry

I have seen many aspiring and successful speakers hold back on claiming their spot on the digital stage, which makes it harder for them to succeed as speakers.

If you are struggling with self-confidence, please remember that there is no one else on the planet with your perspective, life experience, heart aches, or successes. No one else has walked in your shoes and experienced life from your point of view. Not one soul. You are unique, and if you can define your focus and own it digitally, you will become someone people cannot ignore.

Summarizing the Three Starting Points

Define your focus, tie your presence to a powerful *why*, and have the confidence to step into your digital voice, which will lead to more opportunities to use your voice on physical stages. I believe an online presence is the doorway to a professional speaking career today. Don't wait until you're ready to stand on stage. Start now—learn and grow.

Once you have your *why* and your focus nailed down, and you're determined to overcome your fears and embrace this opportunity, read through my list of 16 things you can do right now to get started.

The Next 16 Things on the Digital Stage to Launch Your Speaking Career

1. Share world-class content

The starting point is to share world-class content aligned to your focus. If you want to be a social leader, **creating your own content** is critical. That being said, the vast majority of my time is spent **sharing other people's world-class content**, but *always* with my opinion on why I am sharing it. We need to help people find and spend time with great content, so if you always include your opinion on why you're sharing information, you are already performing better than most people because you're delivering a service.

This is how you draw people to you and your content. Including your own analysis or commentary with everything you share is microblogging and it's very powerful. Make this the mainstay of your content, and you will start to build a solid social leadership position.

And if writing isn't your strong point, it's never been easier to do video. You can also draw, design, share photos, or use other techniques to tell a story.

The only thing that matters is value. The only thing that matters is sharing high-quality information your audience doesn't want to ignore, versus putting content out there just so you'll be seen. Before sharing, ask yourself if it is amazing, inspiring, useful, impactful, and worth your audience's time? If the answer is yes, your posts will stand out.

There are **five reasons people share content:** curiosity, amazement, interest, astonishment, and uncertainty. Keep these in mind when you post, because this is what your audience wants—great quality content that makes an impact and that they will want to pass on to their own audiences.

2. Where do you quench your knowledge thirst?

With your core theme in mind, **identify five to ten publications** that inspire you and align with that theme. Find websites and news sources, subscribe to their emails, follow social pages, and visit them often. Make it a habit to share this content, but remember, *always* offer an opinion on why you are sharing it. Your audience is looking for value and they expect community leaders to flag content that is worth their time. Be of service.

3. Participate – yes, participate!

I see a lot of people pushing information out there, but the vast majority of them are not participating. This is the best way to establish yourself—by commenting, asking questions, and creating conversations on your digital channels. Yes, that is what we're there for, right? Creating conversations. Participate actively, every day, everywhere. Just this will help you become a social leader. It will also help you appreciate the power of social media, because the magic of social media is in the relationships you will build digitally.

4. Integrity is everything

I can verify that none of the C-level business leaders I work find attractive the megaphone approach so common in social media today. When you are a social leader, integrity is everything, especially if you want to get your bosses' support and respect. Don't preach, serve. Don't sell, earn your audience's respect for your knowledge and wisdom. Set a social goal for your social participation.

My own goal is to make people laugh, think, or cry—across all of my social media platforms. Having a very clear goal that becomes the centerpiece of your participation really helps you put a strong stake in the ground in your area of expertise. You also don't get distracted by what others are doing.

5. Build a tribe

I know the term tribe is a bit overused, but that's what we're in the business of doing today—building a tribe! Seth Godin said, "If you're seeking to build awareness, consider building a community instead."[11] To me, this is a tribe.

What is a tribe, then?

> *A social division in a traditional society consisting of families or communities linked by social, economic, religious, or blood ties, with a common culture and dialect, typically having a recognized leader.*[12]

Really think about what this means as you build your tribe. What unites your followers? You are the leader of your own tribe, but it is the collective cooperation that ensures tribes flourish.

6. Audience-focused

While this should be an obvious consideration, most people think about what they want to say versus what their audience wants to hear. Ask your customers: what do you care about? What frightens you today? What are your biggest challenges? How can I help you? Then shape your content to answer those questions. Always, *always* put yourselves in your customer's shoes. That is how you become a world-class social leader.

7. What social platforms should I use?

The answer is always, "Go where your audience is." LinkedIn is critical for any professional, but are Twitter, Instagram, Facebook, and SnapChat relevant to you? What about local platforms like WeChat and Kakao Talk? Be wherever your customers are.

8. Update your relevant social profiles

If LinkedIn is critical, **understand where you are today** at linkedin.com/sales/ssi. Get your Social Selling Index (SSI) measurement, understand where you are in relation to your industry and connections, and set a goal to increase your SSI to sit in the top one percent for your field.

Then **update your profile(s)** and take advantage of the visual opportunity to include a great profile photo and meaningful banner. Also, insert photos, links, and articles throughout your LinkedIn profile—63 percent of the world learns visually, so tell a visual story.

Write an amazing summary on LinkedIn and write it in the first person. Take the time to tell your story and *don't repeat your career*—we can read that in your job profile information. Who are you and what do you care about? Include personal information if you're comfortable. This profile should be good enough that event organizers can use it too.

Under your name on LinkedIn, you have 120 characters to **write your professional headline**. It automatically features your current job title, but why not tell a story? Mine is, "Helping businesses and professionals tell better stories, while rousing passions in people to embrace social leadership." Never miss an opportunity to tell your story and you can use this on other social platforms, such as for your Twitter bio.

9. Hashtags are critical

Get into the **habit of using hashtags**. This links you to ideas and people, and on many platforms, like Twitter and Instagram, you're basically invisible without hashtags. I cannot emphasize enough that hashtags are core to building a profile beyond your immediate network. And yes, even LinkedIn has completely transformed to be driven by hashtags, so use them everywhere.

Here are some suggestions, but the best way to discover the most appropriate hashtags for you is to look at what the top people in your industry are using and then get into the habit of using three in every post. You can use up to ten on Instagram, but for most social platforms, **three should be your maximum.**

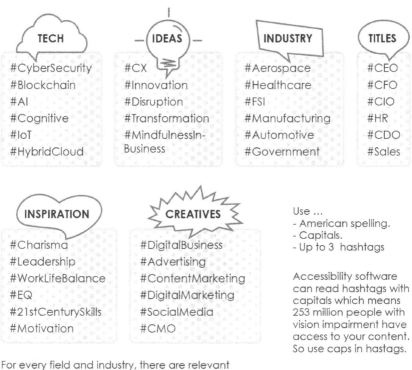

TECH
#CyberSecurity
#Blockchain
#AI
#Cognitive
#IoT
#HybridCloud

IDEAS
#CX
#Innovation
#Disruption
#Transformation
#MindfulnessIn-Business

INDUSTRY
#Aerospace
#Healthcare
#FSI
#Manufacturing
#Automotive
#Government

TITLES
#CEO
#CFO
#CIO
#HR
#CDO
#Sales

INSPIRATION
#Charisma
#Leadership
#WorkLifeBalance
#EQ
#21stCenturySkills
#Motivation

CREATIVES
#DigitalBusiness
#Advertising
#ContentMarketing
#DigitalMarketing
#SocialMedia
#CMO

Use ...
- American spelling.
- Capitals.
- Up to 3 hashtags

Accessibility software can read hashtags with capitals which means 253 million people with vision impairment have access to your content. So use caps in hastags.

For every field and industry, there are relevant hashtags. Check out thought leaders in your field for the ones being used.

Popular hashtags

10. Be present, be consistent

An essential part of building a personal brand **is consistent presence**. You can be present every day, once a week, or once a month—whatever you decide is up to you, although as professional speakers, we should be more active than most people! My advice is to sit down with a coffee on a Sunday morning and schedule your posts for the week. This is a 30-minute exercise to read articles and then share them with your opinion. I use Hootsuite to automate my content, but there are many other options.

Automation is a key part of being successful; it helps you set yourself up for regular sharing and it helps you manage your presence. However, automation can't stand in for presence and community engagement on social media throughout the week. And keep in mind that automated responses (such as on Twitter) will annoy your followers.

11. Grit is king

There is too much talk about shortcuts to success in the social world, and the reality is, if you want to claim your space as a thought leader, you need to make a commitment and be in it for the long haul. I have been doing this for more than a decade, and for nearly eight years, no one was talking back. I kept going, because I really believed in social leadership as the career opportunity and social change opportunity of our time.

Claim your space, but keep going, no matter what. It is getting harder and harder to stand out. However, with integrity and passion at the core, you have more chance to shine through.

12. Be selective about what rules you follow

According to a commonly quoted rule, blogs shouldn't be longer than 400 words. **Rubbish!** The average word count of top-ranking content (in Google) is between 1,140 and 1,285 words, according to SearchMetrics. With Google's increasing focus on quality, longer form content is winning on search rankings.

This is a new world. Focus on being awesome and learn what works for you as you go. The only thing that matters is delivering value to your audience. *Rules are distracting.* Focus on what matters most: being awesome.

13. Don't do too much

We live in the era of content shock and there is so much coming at all of us today! Everyone is overwhelmed and suffering from FOMO![13] At the same time, a constant issue for professionals is the amount of time necessary to succeed on social media. My answer is, do less but always be world-class when you show up.

Don't add to the noise. Add value and a quality of information your audience can't ignore, and you will break through the clutter of infobesity.[14] However, creating your own content is a real time commitment. Start with one blog or video a month, and once you start feeling the benefits, you will naturally make the time to do more. You don't have to do more than you can handle right now. Find *your* starting point and get going.

14. Be positive, be kind, and #THINK

We are living in a time of cataclysmic change on a global scale, when fears and anxieties fill our digital channels. It gets overwhelming some days. However, I believe we gain nothing when we are part of the negative cycle of information. People will switch us off, because we are all getting too much negativity and we don't want to hear it anymore! Sure, we can't help contributing to it sometimes—it's an intense time to be alive—but if you can, be a positive force for good in the world. Your audience will appreciate it.

Keep in mind that there are many trolls online, just waiting to get into an argument. Avoid feeding them. Try to be respectful and don't go into attack mode if you can help it. As a female blogger I have experienced nonsense with trolls, and so will you. Just move on if someone annoys you and never be unkind. It's perfectly acceptable, however, to be cheeky ☺.

Before posting or responding, take a moment to THINK—the perfect acronym.

T – is it True?
H – is it Helpful?
I – is it Inspiring?
N – is it Necessary?
K – is it Kind?

Taking that moment before posting or responding is often all you need to ensure you'll have no regrets. Let's all THINK and elevate the conversation on social media to a kinder place for everyone.

15. Give (#GivingEconomy)

If you want to be a world-class social leader, spend as much time helping others succeed as you spend doing anything else on social media. The more senior or influential you are, the more impactful that is. Succeeding on social media is not a solo sport. It's about all of us coming together, engaging in conversation and supporting each other. Not just the stars, but everyone who is delivering real value to their social networks.

If there are amazing people in your community doing amazing work, help them succeed. You will gain so much more in return with this mindset.[15]

16. Be you

I know authenticity is an overused word today, but it is a must if you want to be a successful social leader. When you are not authentic, it comes through, no matter how you try to hide it. So, tap into your deepest self, share your passion for your topic, and don't get distracted by all of the other noise going on around you. It's so easy to get distracted or to let the voice in your head tell you you're not good enough. Push it all aside and go for it. The more authentic and genuine you are, the more people will trust what you have to say.

Remember:

> Don't sell, share.
> Don't pitch, serve.

I have built my entire business on this philosophy and I know it works. If you have a dream to stand on the physical stage, get started now with the digital stage. It will open the door to your dreams. Embrace it and enjoy it. Good luck.

If you take three things away, I hope they are...

- Start by getting **insanely focused.** The riches are always in the niches, so focus is the first and most important part of building a social leadership position.
- Then be committed to **delivering excellence** every time you show up. The only way to be world class is to always have a world-class mindset when you participate on social media.
- And finally, **be of service.** One of the most important things you can do is make serving your audience your priority, because whether you're speaking or on the digital stage, it's not about you, it's never been about you. It's always about your audience.

The best way to sell something: don't sell anything. Earn the awareness, respect, and trust of those who buy. —Rand Fishkin, founder, Moz

---

1   https://seths.blog/2018/09/what-are-you-organizing/
2   https://en.oxforddictionaries.com/definition/tribe
3   https://www.urbandictionary.com/define.php?term=Fomo
4   https://www.urbandictionary.com/define.php?term=Infobesity
5   Here's a blog I wrote recently to illustrate this point. https://www.linkedin.com/pulse/2019-lets-support-drivers-givers-change-agents-andrea-edwards/

Andrea Edwards

Andrea Edwards, the Digital Conversationalist, is a globally award-winning B2B communications professional, evangelist, and expert in content marketing, social leadership, personal branding, and employee advocacy. These four focus areas—all connected under the umbrella of communication—fundamentally transform how we do business. When we lead socially, it empowers us to delight customers, grow our careers, and lead our industries.

A content marketing strategy pioneer, blogger, writer, speaker, and trainer/coach for businesses and professionals around the world, Andrea is a regular speaker at industry events, and she consults with the world's largest companies on the internal transformation needed to maximize business growth in our digital future.

For more in claiming your digital stage and being a social leader: www.AndreaTEdwards.com

Authentically Speaking

by Mette Johansson

Good speakers are passionate about sharing a message to benefit the world. Great speakers touch upon something at the core of the hearts of the audience to move them to action.

There are techniques to help you get from being a good speaker to a great speaker. For instance, captivating storytelling appeals to emotions and is a great way to win your audience over. However, authenticity is the best way to become an *outstanding* speaker.

From Good to Great Speeches

In the best-selling book *Good to Great*, James C. Collins describes a recipe for business success that involves exploring questions including:

- what you are passionate about,
- what your company is great at, and

- what drives your business's economic engine, or in other words, what is the value that you bring to satisfy people's needs or wants.

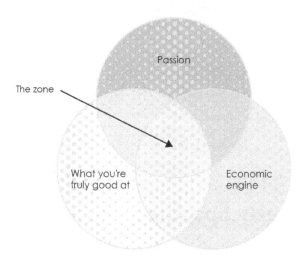

Sweet spot for your business

This recipe is also applicable to creating effective speeches. If you hit the sweet spot where these three areas overlap, you'll have a great topic and you will be able to present it authentically.

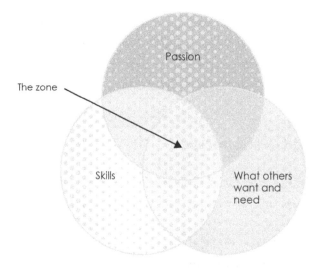

Sweet spot for your keynote

In this chapter, we will look at how you get to this sweet spot: how you find topics that will inspire your audience and make a lasting impact.

Your Passion Derives from Your Values

In the context of business, I define passion as a strong desire or enthusiasm for something. With my coaching clients, I have observed that a passion will be a long-lived one when it is based on your values. Let me give you an example: I have a strong enthusiasm for art, but it doesn't translate into a long-lived passion. It is not based on, or linked to, one of my core values.

On the other hand, I value personal and professional growth, both for others and myself. This has led me to a very strong passion for speaking, training, coaching, and mentoring—four different means for guiding others to become a better version of themselves.

Let's begin with your personal values. We're not talking about the values that your country holds, or those associated with your religion. We're not talking about your family's values, and definitely not about the corporate values of the organization you work for. It's about what's fundamentally important to *you*.

I work with many different groups of people to help them find their values. I find it interesting that when I work with executives from the corporate world, more often than not they find it difficult to tell me what they're passionate about. When I present to groups of 25 or 50 executives and ask, "Who knows their personal values?" often, only one person in the room can describe these to me in a few words.

In contrast, when I work with entrepreneurs or groups of women, they tend to have a much higher awareness of their own values. With female leaders, typically one-third of the room can, on the spot, list three to five core values.[1] In a group of entrepreneurs, it is not unusual for half or two-thirds of participants to raise their hands to share their values.[2] This leads to my strong belief that women are, on average, more driven by values and purpose than men. Women: use this on stage! And to everyone else: why not use the passion advantage, too?

Do you know your values? If you're not clear on your values, do this free online test[3] to help you clarify them and continue to explore your "inner theme," as speaker Fredrik Härén calls it—the topic that is easy for you to speak about authentically.

After doing the test, write down your values.

Look at the values you defined. What ties them together? What are you enthusiastic about that fits these values?

If you want to be authentic on stage take a moment to connect the dots in your life—perhaps with a coach—and find your topic and the message to the world that resonates the most with you. I promise you, if it resonates strongly with you, it will be based on your values.

Using Your Strengths

During an entrepreneur-mentoring course in 2013, I was staring at a piece of paper with a pencil-drawn mountain on it. The instructor told us that we're all sitting on a mountain of value and asked us to write down all our achievements. I had left corporate life a few months earlier and, after 15 minutes, the sheet of paper was still blank. I didn't see anything that could amount to a tiny hill, let alone a tall mountain. I hadn't reached the top during my corporate career; I'd received no awards. This is a typical female perspective, and nowhere is this way of looking at achievements more ubiquitous than in corporate life. Besides, being Danish, I was raised with the cultural rule that I was not to think I'm anyone special or that I'm better than anyone else.

Since that moment in 2013 I have discovered that I *do* stand on a mountain of value. There are things I am better at than other people. Luckily, there are also loads of things that other people are better at than me! We're all special.

1. Knowledge

In this context, I'd like you to focus on the knowledge that comes from studying, gathering information, and reading books.

One of my mentors once said that you only need to read three books on a topic to become an expert. I'm not claiming that this is true for all topics and audiences—however, do consider the importance of reading three different books with different views on a topic. Let's take happiness. The happiness business has been booming in this millennium, and the recipes for success vary widely. By reading and reflecting on the three best books on this subject, you'll have more knowledge than 99 percent of the population.

Combine it with your own experience—see segment number four below—or interview a few dozen people on their views on the topic; that's how you can make their experience *your* experience. If you listen to your audiences when you start speaking, you'll soon be a thought leader.

Consider: In what areas do you have more knowledge than the majority of people, or is there a gap you can fill by reading three books to fill out your expertise?

2. Identity, or DNA

Every person has a unique combination of skills, knowledge, and experience—a certain "DNA" that makes us interesting.

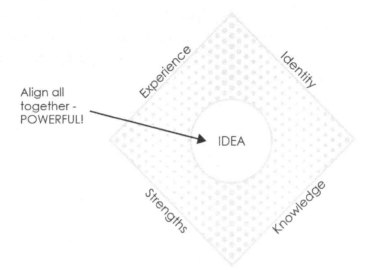

Align all together - POWERFUL!

Experience

Identity

IDEA

Strengths

Knowledge

Your Identity, or DNA

In 2018, I attended a talk by New Zealander Cam Calkoen, who was born with cerebral palsy, a condition that affects his ability to walk and talk. There were two things he wanted as a child: to be an athlete and to be a speaker. He became both, and now he earns his living through speaking. According to Calkoen, he took his difficulty talking—what others saw as an impediment to a career in professional speaking—and turned it into an asset. He uses his unique identity to inspire others to pursue human excellence and dream big.

Consider: What is your special DNA, or identity, and how can you change it into an asset?

3. Talent and skills

Knowledge is what you know about—say, marketing. Skills are what you can do—for instance, making a strategic marketing plan. Knowledge is what makes you a thought leader. Skills can give you credibility for being a thought leader on a topic, but you don't need to look far beyond the many gurus on leadership to see that knowledge even without skills can lead to a position of thought leadership.

Your talent and the skills you've developed throughout your life are the third piece in your strengths puzzle. Maybe you're trained in finance; maybe you're a designer or an entrepreneur. We often take the skills we've developed for granted or dismiss them as "nothing special." No wonder. If you work in a bank, you're surrounded by other financial experts; if you're a designer, there will be better-known designers than you; if you're an entrepreneur, the media is full of star-status entrepreneurs who seem to have success with everything they touch.

I want you to keep two things in mind. First, you may not see that you're special because there are many people that share your abilities. You don't see the wood for the trees. Second, your talent and skills are only one piece of the strengths puzzle. When you take that piece and add the other pieces, it becomes your unique puzzle that nobody else in the world can claim.

Imagine: If you were in a completely different field or industry with your current skills, which of your talents and skills would stand out?

4. Experience

Like your skills, your experience seems normal to you because that's all you've known in your life so far. Once at a party, someone I was talking to introduced himself as having lived in seven countries. I thought for a little while, silently considered my countries of residence and said, "I guess my number is 11." The rest of the evening, I kept hearing people say, "Is she the one who has lived in 11 countries?"

I moved abroad when I was two years old and followed a course of international studies, and I have lived in international communities my entire adult life, so I did not think that this would be worth mentioning. To you, this idea may seem far-fetched. To me, changing countries is normal, and all I have known in my life.

I hear similar stories from such people as the woman who started her first company as a teenager; or the one who became a competitive golf player in her 40s, two years after picking up a golf club for the first time; or the first black women to break out of her community and enter a prestigious university. Those are all interesting and unique experiences that make for fascinating and inspiring stories, but people living them don't see them as anything special.

The good news is: if you, against all odds, haven't experienced anything that's unique in your life, you can go out and create your unique experience right now. You can eat your way through all the Asian countries; you can ride a bicycle along the entire coast of Australia; you can interview 100 people on their secret for a happy life. You're in charge of your experiences.

Reflect: What are your experience "woods" that you don't see for the trees? Can you create any?

Combining Knowledge, Identity, Talent and Skills, and Experience

Look at some of the TED speakers who have seven-digit views online. You'll see that many made their stories unique by using selected pieces— or all the pieces—of their strength puzzle. Take "My Stroke of Insight" by Jill Bolte Taylor, a brain expert (*knowledge*) who suffered a stroke and survived to share the *experience*. Or lawyer Susan Cain, who started writing and speaking for introverts, reflecting her own personality, or *identity*. One of my favorite TED speakers, Nigerian novelist Chimamanda Ngozi Adichie, realized early on that she was unique in her combination of knowledge, identity, talent, and experience. As an early and passionate reader, she realized how books with children playing in the snow were quite different to her daily reality, and valuing her own experience allowed her to create a new niche.

What People Want to Hear

In *Good to Great*, Collins describes the third circle of success as being about what drives your economic engine. It's about how you add value to your customers. Translated to a speaking context: what do people want to hear? What do they want to spend 18 minutes or an hour of their time listening to? How can you make a positive impact on their lives, their mindset, or their careers? If you want to be a professional speaker, there is the additional challenge of what people are willing to *pay* to listen to.

This is where the importance of your ideas comes in, or "ideas worth spreading," as TED Talks, the new standard for public speaking, puts it in their slogan.

Adding value is standard for everything you want to sell. Whether it's a new skincare line or a keynote talk, people pay you to solve a problem for them, or to fulfill their wants and needs.

Finding out what people want to hear about is easy. Discuss your ideas with friends, new people you meet, or your clients. Do they light up and ask questions or do they yawn and find a way to change the conversation? As a next step, suggest your idea as a keynote talk to associations, conferences, or events that cater to the people that you help.

Is Being Authentic on Stage an Oxymoron?
Trust comes on foot and leaves on horseback.

When I read this Dutch proverb, I see horses galloping in all directions. Edelman, which does annual surveys on trust, states that the 2018 survey "reveals a world of seemingly stagnant distrust."[4] In the past decade, whether in business or politics or academia, trust has been eroding.

This is a problem, because trust is the glue of society. It's a fundamental necessity in business. Look at brands: we buy them because we expect that we can trust them.

Where there's a problem, there's an opportunity. You can be trustworthy, and people will turn to you because, as the same studies show, people are hungry for leaders they can trust. Within the complex mechanism of trust, congruency and credibility are central elements. And this is where authenticity comes in.

Consistently putting on a persona that is not you may be your strategy to be perceived as credible. However, in the long run it's very difficult to consistently put on a mask, and many people are perceptive enough to see through it.

A far more sustainable strategy to seem credible is being authentic, even when you're acting and talking on stage.

The term "authenticity" is often used casually, without a common understanding of what it means. To me, it's being true to *your* values. Most people will intuitively perceive you as being authentic—or inauthentic—based on how consistently you live your values.

This means that unless one of your core values is to show how you *truly* feel at all times, you *may* pretend to be confident on stage, even when you're not. Focus on sharing messages that stem from your values. If your message is, for example, about being courageous, and this is a central part of your value system, it makes sense that you pick up all the courage you've got and pretend to be confident, even though you have butterflies in your tummy. The audience does not judge you on your confidence, but on your core value of courage.

Confidence is not a deep personality trait; it's a skill we can learn. It's OK to "fake it till you make it". When you step out of your comfort zone; you're practicing a skill to grow.

What you want to be genuine about are your values. Values are what is most important to you in your life—what you truly believe in, and what you stand for. When you show congruency on this deeper level, regardless of your skillset, people will see you as genuine.

For instance, if you talk about the importance of change, being authentic means that you value and live flexibility and that you're open to do things differently when the situation calls for it. To use my own example, I arranged for Denise Morris Kipnis to deliver her signature talk, "The Three Change Myths." On that particular rainy Friday afternoon, only a third of the people who signed up actually showed up and we held the talk in a different room than planned. A few things beyond her control had changed, yet she still went ahead with it as if it was nothing. She lived the value of flexibility and she excelled. The audience responded that her talk was both very professional and authentic.

In contrast, I attended a presentation by a famous proponent of mindfulness. He spoke about the need for mindfulness and, at the same time, he expressed deep anger about how Coca Cola is spoiling society, and how Coca Cola is responsible for the adverse effects of sugar, including diabetes and obesity. Without being able to pinpoint it, the audience noticed that something was not quite right. The more anger he expressed toward Coca Cola, the more his credibility on mindfulness diminished. Balance—which is incongruent with anger—is key to mindfulness. When people discover in their subconscious minds that you don't value or live balance, your perception of authenticity in the area of mindfulness is at stake. The audience gets the vague suspicion that you're not a true believer of what you're preaching.

Being Authentic on Stage

Being authentic on stage goes beyond showing a picture of your family on a slide. All this does is give the audience a glimpse into one of your other roles. Sure, the audience does appreciate putting a face on a leader,[5] but it doesn't go far enough. In fact, if you as a woman talking to bankers about the need for change in the financial industry show a family photograph, you may be seen first as a mother and second as the expert that you are. This may be an obstacle to achieving what you set out to achieve—making a difference in the financial world. And it is not inauthentic to focus on the side of your personality most relevant in that situation: being a professional. In this professional setting, your authenticity depends on your professionalism.

What's core to being authentic on stage is staying true to your values. This in turn requires that you're comfortable with your values, that you embody them, and that you have made it a habit to live them on a daily basis. When you've reached that point, you will continue living them when you step in front of a microphone, too.

When you speak about inclusive leadership, you'll only be seen by others as being inclusive if you live values such as curiosity and respect— curiosity and respect for people whatever their skin color, gender, sexual orientation, ability, and other traits. When you speak about embracing failure, you'd better be OK when there are technical difficulties with your slides.

Three Key Takeaways

- Before your next keynote talk: consider what your values are and ensure that everything you say and do in your talk is congruent with them. Think ahead about ways that you can let your true values shine through on stage.
- Authentic speakers touch upon something core in the hearts of the audience: their values. If you base your talk on your values, you'll attract people with the same value system. You'll be inspired, and you will inspire your audience to follow you and your advice as a thought leader. It's the recipe to become an outstanding speaker.
- Speaking on stage will mean you change the way you normally speak. If you want the audience's attention, you will act things out. This is not being inauthentic—it is adapting to the situation. What makes you authentic is showing what you're passionate about. You let your beliefs shine through and you live your values.

1   If you're stumbling over the math because executives could both be women and men, know that groups of senior leaders sadly often include very few women. Sometimes, there are no women represented.
2   Entrepreneurs whose original idea is based on passion have a higher chance of success. Passion nourishes drive, and drive is essential to starting a business.
3   http://learning.metamindtraining.com/
4   https://www.edelman.com/trust-barometer
5   See Edelman Trust Barometer, 2016

Mette Johansson

Mette Johansson, an internationally renowned author, keynote speaker, and award-winning entrepreneur. She worked in leadership roles for multinational corporations across the globe for 15 years before founding MetaMind Training, a training consultancy providing highly customized learning programs on people skills such authentic leadership, presenting with impact, and intercultural intelligence.

Mette has internationally presented her signature keynote on how to become an authentic leader—the leader who we follow not because of their position, wealth, or title, but because we are inspired to follow them.

A recipient of *Insight Magazine*'s 50 Most Promising Women in Business award, Mette is the founder, relentless driver, and Chair for KeyNote, a nonprofit online directory of female speakers, she is on a mission to bring diversity to stages around the world.

For more on authenticity: www.MetteJohansson.com

Building Credibility as a Professional Speaker – What it takes to turn speaking into a profession

by Natalie Turner

I was eight years old the first time I gave a speech. I was standing on the street outside WHSmith newsagent, part of the weekly outreach team from our local church in England. The wind was howling and people were focused on shopping, not listening to a young girl share a message about love and hope and making a difference. A few people stopped to listen, probably more intrigued by a child's echoing voice than by the actual content of what I was saying, but in that moment I was amazed by the power that words could have on people, to stop them in their tracks, to hold their attention, to maybe even change their behavior and inspire them to do something different. Little did I know that one day I would become a professional speaker, that those early years of watching preachers, my parents included, and practicing the craft of speaking to audiences would be the starting point of an apprenticeship to build the two fundamental building blocks of credibility. Those building blocks are what you say—the content of your message—and how you say it—your voice, your body language, and your ability to engage others and inspire authority. But these are not enough. How do you build this credibility in the first place, so that people can see you and hear your message?

You may have an inspiring and relevant speech and you can speak with passion and confidence, but what does it really take to turn speaking into a profession? How do you amplify your message beyond your voice, so that you start to attract the right opportunities, connections, and audiences? In this chapter I will share what I mean by being professional and outline strategies that I hope will support and guide you in your quest to become a professional speaker.

First of all, what does it mean to be professional? The word can have many different meanings, including:

- Looking and acting in a professional manner
- Conforming to the specific ethics and standards of your industry
- Being engaged in an activity as your paid occupation rather than as an amateur

All three are important to being a professional, but what does world-class look like? How can you reach the global stage?

Let's take each of these questions in turn.

Looking and Acting Professional

For us to look professional, we have to believe we are professional. This requires a mindset of confidence and self-belief. It is no good starting a marketing campaign around your keynote if you don't really believe that you can do it or that anyone will want to hire you. Sadly, I think this is one of the biggest stumbling blocks that women encounter when they consider going pro. They think they don't know enough and are not good enough, even though they probably have put in the practice hours and are even experts in their fields. You have got to want this. You have got to believe that you can do it—not in an arrogant way, but yes, with assertiveness and ambition, attributes that women often feel uncomfortable demonstrating.

What is the difference between being an amateur, who speaks to audiences for free, and making speaking part of your professional working life? Money. Getting paid. You will only look and act professionally and command professional fees once you start to believe you are a professional.

There are a couple of points worth discussing on being paid before we move on. If you are a professional speaker and someone asks you to speak for free, what do you do? First, think of the upside and marketing reach it will give you. Is it the right audience? Will the organizers market you actively in their advertising? Will they provide you with video footage, photographs and endorsements? Don't just do it for free. Make sure the value exchange they're proposing benefits you as well as them. To use myself as an example, I chose to speak at Harvard's HPAIR conference in Manila because of the brand association with Harvard University, and at the Innov8ers conference in Bangkok because it was a plenary keynote where we created a marketing partnership that reached out to over 25,000 people—extraordinary exposure for my message.

What we have to remember is professionals get paid, and if all speakers start speaking for free then we dilute the value of the service that we provide and make it harder for other people to become professional. Thankfully, the speaking industry is quite a lucrative one and is growing. As we build our personal brands, we also want to make sure we are adding the most value we can at the industry level.

1. Conforming to industry ethics and standards
I have been speaking professionally for 13 years. One of the things I wish I had done earlier is join a speaking association. This will accelerate

your development as a professional. I am a member of APSS (Asia Pacific Speakers Singapore). Meetups are informative, practical, and educational. It is here you really learn to hone the tools of the trade. It is here that you mingle with other speakers who are grappling with similar challenges. It is here you meet with people who are veterans in the industry whom you can learn from, look up to, and emulate. You will also learn that speaking as a profession has certain protocols and codes of conduct.

If you aren't pro yet, choose associate membership or, if you can provide evidence of speaker earnings, become a professional member. This opens a number of developmental pathways open to you, including becoming a globally recognized Certified Speaking Professional (CSP). Speaking associations will also advertise local and global conferences, which are great places to make connections and to learn and develop professionalism.

2. Engaging in a specific activity as a paid occupation

How do you get engaged as a paid speaker? There are a variety of routes to market, as a speaker, to earn professional fees. You can use speaker bureaus, which take a commission for a speaking engagement that they make on your behalf, and personal proactive outreach to raise your credibility. But before you run off to join professional bureaus or start advertising yourself, you need to get some fundamentals in place.

These include:

1. A compelling website that people can visit to learn more about you and your message and, most importantly, see you in action. Or, if speaking is part of a broader professional suite of services that you provide, make sure that you have a separate page dedicated to your work as a speaker.
2. A short video, or showreel, that shows you in a number of different situations speaking to people. It can also include short

testimonials and a more intimate profile of you sharing about what inspires you to be a speaker.

Please remember, these elements don't need to be perfect. Another trait I find common in women is they think everything has to be absolutely perfect before they start to promote themselves. It will never be perfect, and in fact it shouldn't be. You will change and improve. You will design new videos and you will learn new skills and better ways of doing things.

Think of yourself, and your speech, as a product. Like any good product, you have to have attributes that make you valuable. You also need a marketing strategy for how you are going to reach the audiences that you wish to engage.

For starters, think through:

1. **Your value propositions.** What are the challenges and interests of your audience? What is the value that you think that you offer them? Make it clear in your marketing collateral.
2. **Your brand attributes.** What do you want people to feel or experience after having listened to you? If you want to be authentic, ask people what they think, and listen to the feedback that you receive. You can also use brand identification tools such as 360Reach and then design your brand around the attributes that people perceive in your current behavior. What do you want people to remember you for?
3. **Your market.** Who are your buyers? Many speakers immediately think of the organizers of conferences specific to their area of expertise. More often than not, conference organizers will ask you to speak for free or pay as a sponsor. While you may meet a potential client in the audience after you have spoken, most people I know who speak at conferences do it for the exposure it will give their brand. There are many other buyers to consider,

such as industry and trade associations and conferences run by organizations for their employees.

The latter is the market that I predominantly focus on. This means that I speak to business audiences who bring their employees together for an internal conference. Invariably, event and conference organizers will look for an opening and closing keynote speaker. They also have event budgets. So, how do you reach these buyers?

Be visible where you will attract new contacts. For me, that means being visible and authoritative through the use of content marketing on social media and podcasts and in the business press. My preference is LinkedIn, through which I have had numerous enquiries. I have found it to be one of the best forms of outreach for business development. It is also a publishing platform. As a writer, I can write and publish articles and include links to events that I am hosting or co-hosting with partners, which add value to people's knowledge and open up doors for further engagement.

I am also an author. I cannot over-emphasize the benefits of being an author of a credible book on your subject of expertise. Since I published my book *Yes, You Can Innovate*, my business—both my professional speaking and my consultancy and training business—has grown exponentially and globally, and it continues to do so. You can package your book and your speech together at events, keynotes, training programs, corporate purchases, and more. It also gives you credible authority as a thought leader and thinker in the space in which you operate.

Be busy asking for referrals through reaching out to your own and other people's networks. Again, LinkedIn is an excellent platform for this. Be genuinely interested in building relationships with people who will engage in your area of interest and expertise. Gone are the days where people can blast out advertising and expect people to buy, show up, or engage. Like any good relationship building, it is about contacting people, finding mutual common interests, and offering and receiving value. We are genuinely trying to share with people something that will pique their interest and meet their needs.

> **Three Key Takeaways**
>
> Building credibility as a professional speaker—what it takes to turn speaking into a paid profession—can be summarized in three key main points:
>
> - Believe and act as a professional.
> - Join and be part of the regional and global professional industry.
> - Treat yourself and your keynote speech as a product and service that adds value by building credibility through professional relationship development.

More than forty years on, I remember that younger version of me speaking on the streets on a Saturday morning—even when I am on the stage standing in front of corporate business people. It was then that the spark for what I do now was ignited. It was there that I started to build confidence and the early seeds of credibility. It has been a journey. You need to put in the hours and practice, practice, and practice. You need to be an amateur before you are a professional. Develop your message, build your self-belief, learn the tools of the trade, and start to reach out. The world needs to hear your voice, and it's up to you to give them reasons to believe.

Natalie Turner

Natalie Turner is an international speaker on innovation and leadership. She is the CEO of the Entheo Network, the inventor of the *6 'T's® of Innovation,* and the founder of Women Who Lead, a coaching and luxury retreat service for women in leadership. Natalie is the author of *Yes, You Can Innovate: Discover your innovation strengths and develop your creative potential.*

For more on innovation and creativity: http://Natalie-Turner.net/

PART 3

WHAT COMES AFTERWARDS:

Getting booked, relationships,
negotiating, and the business
side of professional speaking

Speaking for Social Impact

by Lauren Sorkin, Managing Director, 100 Resilient Cities

I've learned that people will forget what you said, people will forget what you did, but people will never forget how you made them feel. —Maya Angelou

My career is dedicated to social impact, or the effects an individual's or organizations' actions can have on the well-being of the community. From my first job working to promote emerging clean technologies with the European Union's Environment Directorate General to my work today as the managing director for the Rockefeller Foundation's 100 Resilient Cities in Asia Pacific, my personal and professional missions have been constant: to understand our society's greatest challenges and to use my time and energy to ameliorate them. Taking on societal challenges means motivating people to work with me every step of the way. And that is just the beginning. To achieve social impact, people need to go beyond either identifying with or feeling sympathetic towards an issue I present, to taking collective action.

Starting out, I used public speaking opportunities to mobilize coalitions on specific projects. Today, in an increasingly interconnected world supported by mobile technology, I use my words as a catalyst to enable others to work toward goals we share even if we've never met.

This is my story…

Taking the Plunge

The year is 2007 and, as a recent post-graduate, I am standing in front of a room of 80 people in a small town in Peru's Sacred Valley. My hands shake as I hold the notes for the first speech I will make since landing my dream job as the knowledge management lead for the Initiative for Conservation in the Andean Amazon (ICAA). I realize that this is my chance to inspire the incredibly busy, savvy, and well-connected leaders from across the region to trust me and my colleagues to organize their collective experiences and resources for a proposed three-year collaboration. And I must do this in my second language, Spanish.

When planning the speech, I realized that I had more questions than I had answers. Though I had surveyed each of the groups individually about their learning priorities, this was the first time we were coming together. I knew the purpose of the initiative, but our project management team did not have a clear path to get there. Over the course of that speech, I reflected on the enormous opportunity we had if we shared knowledge about how to conserve priority landscapes within the Andean Amazon and I called out the abilities of each of the organizations in the room to contribute to that vision. I ended the speech with an invitation to co-create and manage goals within a framework—a series of workshops and a website that we had created to support the program.

My speech and those of my colleagues were a success because we achieved our organization's objectives for that day. We made every person in the room feel important, feel valued, and feel welcome as a contributor to our initiative. The speeches opened a very heated dialogue between the regional leaders about how to move from shared aspirations to collective action. We gave the leaders a platform to connect the purpose of their respective organizations to a common set of goals. Over the next six months, three working groups formed and outlined specific work plans to improve sustainability of a massive infrastructure investment program in the region, improve natural product and tourism certification, and promote indigenous peoples' involvement in economic activities in the region. The program was so successful that it was extended to five years, and many of the coalitions fortified by the program endure to this day.[21]

I have continued to refine the speaking lessons I learned from ICAA across five continents. I'll share them here to help you improve the well-being of the communities you hold most dear.

The Quick View – How to Design a Keynote to Promote Social Impact

Speaking to inspire impact requires three things:

- Connecting to the human—emotionally, physically, or both
- Connecting to purpose—express a vision, a clear articulation of shared values, or an outcome that inspires
- Connecting to people—explain your role and the roles others could play

Break Through the Noise and Connect to the Human

Look around most conference rooms today and you'll see that half the audience members are hunched over, staring at their phones. As speakers in today's mobile-enabled world, we need to keep in mind that people can filter out unwanted content, and unfortunately, filter us out as well. To break through increasing competition and noise, we need to introduce our issues by appealing to people on a human level and speaking to their emotional and physical selves. We need to be able to paint a picture of the challenge with a compelling and relatable story, outstanding visuals, and—if you can—through some physical movement.

Floods in Manila

When I worked for the Asian Development Bank in Manila in 2009, the city was hit by hurricane Ketsana or, as it was known locally, Typhoon Ondoy. The storm wreaked havoc on the city and shut it down for most of a week. Seven hundred and forty-seven souls lost their lives and the government calculated over a billion dollars in damages. For weeks the press was flooded with images of familiar streets under more than six feet of water and neighbors being evacuated from their houses in rafts.

My colleagues and I discussed these images, our experiences, and our desire to respond to climate change. This was a natural way to start discussions about the increasingly severe impacts of climate change across developing Asia and the need for all of our investments to both respond to the predicted impacts of climate change and to actively reduce greenhouse gas emissions. Within months of leading the completion of ADB's assessment of how to respond to climate change across the five sub-regions of the Bank,[22] we'd formed a diverse Climate Change Community of Practice, staffed by a coalition of investment officers from across every sector and operational department. Members of this group provided support to each other to meet ambitious goals for lending to mitigate climate change, including beating ADB's $2 billion clean energy investment target.

Often you will need to grab the attention of people who don't know you or your cause well. In these cases, in addition to bringing focus to the issues with visuals, it can be very useful to connect to people through some physical movement that makes you and your voice their true focus of attention.

At the APEC Sustainable Urban Development Forum in Chengdu, PRC, I was given an opportunity to address leading Chinese officials interested in understanding how to build resilience in their cities. The audience of over a hundred was listening to me through a simultaneous translation service. I knew it was going to be a struggle to capture their attention and help them understand and engage with resilience concepts.

As I began my remarks, I asked the audience members to stand up and turn to introduce themselves to one person, then sit down again. I explained that with one simple, low-cost intervention, I had just achieved multiple benefits or a "resilience dividend." By reflecting on the challenge of delivering a speech after lunch and in another language to a crowd of relative strangers, I had designed an effective strategy to address multiple problems with a single intervention that created social cohesion between audience members, got their blood flowing (thereby delivering health benefits to the audience), and increased their attentiveness to my presentation by energizing them through simple movements. I then explained that to build resilience in cities they had to take a similar approach: understand their challenges and the relationship between their challenges, and then design singular interventions to address multiple challenges at once.

Connect to Purpose – Creating Shared Visions for Overcoming Challenges.

The core of an effective keynote to mobilize for social impact is a clearly identified purpose. Can you explain to your audiences why they should care, and then how they can act to achieve social impact?

When I started working for 100 Resilient Cities four years ago, urban planning and policy were in the public spotlight. The UN had just published reports calling attention to the fact that more than 50 percent of the global population was already living in cities and that by 2030, two-thirds of humanity will be urban citizens. Moreover, my region of focus, Asia and the Pacific, was in need of upwards of $1.7 trillion in infrastructure investment.[23] My colleagues at 100 Resilient Cities and I were able to call government, private sector, and civil society partners to act on this once-in-a-lifetime opportunity to make urban investments that delivered multiple benefits.

Outlining the scope of the challenge, or presenting the state of the community that is facing a challenge, is a critical first step. Give well-researched, high-level information, then move quickly to describe challenges on a more relatable scale.

When I speak about urbanization in Asia and the Pacific, I say that city systems cannot keep pace with the current rate of people moving into regional cities every month. While "trillions of dollars of investment that could target the poor and vulnerable" is an appropriate and attention-grabbing statistic to use, as a speaker I must quickly move from this level to one that is relatable as a solution. For most audience members outside of the financial sector, mobilizing billions, let alone trillions of dollars is outside of the realm of possibility. So, when I talk about these issues I'm careful to move quickly from outlining the challenge to articulating possible, non-abstract solutions.

Setting the Target – What are the Qualities of Your Response?

When I speak about urban resilience, I always define the subject as: "the ability of citizens, businesses and institutions to survive, adapt, and thrive no matter what kind of shock or stress they face." This is a bold and ambitious target, so it's imperative for me to then explain in specific terms what this means. In Wellington, the city and national governments share the city's spaces with a diverse community and many of New Zealand's top businesses. The city is extremely prone to earthquakes and has only one major water supply line. During the preparation of the city's resilience strategy, the fact that this water supply line runs parallel to the fault became a focus of resilience design efforts. Scenarios indicated that when a large-scale earthquake hits the city, as is expected to happen in the coming decades, citizens could be without water for upwards of 12 weeks.

Working effectively on urban resilience means that when you identify a problem, you don't immediately rush to solve it. Instead, you examine the underlying drivers of the problem and how they will impact your city, both in the short and long term. Wellingtonians set a vision that as the city changes, everyone will survive and thrive. To achieve such a vision, a community must be engaged to ensure projects and investments meet their ongoing needs.

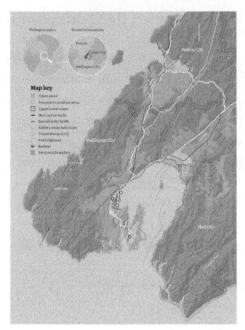

Fault and water lines

Having identified their vulnerability, Wellington designed a system of water bore holes throughout the city. Rather than do this with the water department alone, the city conducted consultations throughout the city and came up with a water station map and design that benefits the city every day of the year, not just in times of trouble. More than 20 water stations are now at trailheads, schools, and community parks and there is one within a one-kilometer walk of everyone in the city. By designing in a way that helps individuals and the community to access emergency services as well as enjoy clean water for recreation, Wellington demonstrates resilience in a way that is easy to explain.

Connect to People – Roles and Real Life! For Who by Whom?

Finally, it's critical that you specifically identify a role for your audience to play in the vision of a better future—there can be no social impact without leaders and first movers. Understand who you are speaking to and what you want audience members to do when they leave the room.

Never have I worked harder as a public speaker than I did on July 24, 2018 in Sydney, Australia. Sydney developed a comprehensive resilience strategy bringing together the 32 councils in the metropolitan area for the first time. This was possible with the support of 100 Resilient Cities and an incredible amount of engagement by the city's intrepid chief resilience officer, Beck Dawson. When it came time to release the strategy, Beck designed a series of four events in one day, and for each one both she and I spoke to a different group of people. First, we spoke to financiers from Australia's major banks and insurance companies and from the UN. Second, we spoke to Sydney's mayors and to CEOs across the 32 councils. And, finally, we spoke to members of the organizations who had pledged support to implement the various initiatives.

In these four briefings, lasting about two hours each, our core messages were the same. I "connected to humans" by telling stories about the major urbanization challenges around the globe, and how they are similar to Sydney's challenges. Then I "connected to purpose" by sharing details about the innovative responses outlined in Strategy Sydney's projects. What was different about each of the briefings was how I connected to the people. In the briefing with the financiers, I spoke more about other examples of how financiers have provided credit for cities that are designing better, more resilient urban centers and asked the participants to do the same. In the briefing with the mayors and CEOs, I spoke about the importance of their leadership and partnership with one another to execute the strategy, specifying examples from across the city. And in the briefing with participant organizations, I applauded their efforts to date and called on them to take part in specific additional projects.

None of this would have been possible without a deep understanding of the context in the city, and of how the people in the room relate to the work. It's critical to think about how your audience relates to your subject and to tailor your calls to action to their specific backgrounds, capacities, and ambitions.

Three Key Takeaways

Connecting to humans:

- Bring people into the present by connecting to their bodies through physical or emotional triggers. I recommend doing this at beginning and end of your presentation so that people sit up and pay attention, and then leave feeling inspired.
- Use eye contact to engage with the audience. If it's a large crowd, make sure you direct attention to all parts of the room.

Connecting to purpose—express a vision, a clear articulation of shared values, or an outcome that inspires:

- Clearly explain why you are advocating for social action. Explain the challenge using facts relevant to your audience.
- Outline a response to the challenge that can be achieved through social action. Invite others to share your vision and a sense of purpose.

Connecting to people:

- Your role—clearly state how you relate to the issue. Are you a leader, a coach, a technical expert, a broker? Explain why you are playing this role. And remember, it's OK to show vulnerability.
- Others' roles—outline possible roles for those in your audience. Don't be afraid to ask for help in areas where you see gaps in capacity.

---

1   https://rmportal.net/library/content/
     the-initiative-for-conservation-in-the-andean-amazon-icaa
2   https://www.preventionweb.net/files/13813_Brochure.pdf
3   Asian Development Bank, 2017

Lauren Sorkin

Lauren Sorkin is Managing Director in Asia Pacific for 100 Resilient Cities, leading an interdisciplinary team working in 12 countries and 21 cities between Pune, India and Wellington, New Zealand. Before joining 100RC, Lauren worked for the Asian Development Bank directing the development of ADB's first Climate Change Implementation Plan and the integration of climate resilience into the Bank's $7 billion portfolio in Vietnam. Lauren also worked for USAID, with the European Commission, and with the Worldwatch Institute, where she published work on biofuels, trans-boundary water management, and infant mortality. She is a proud alumnus of Tufts University and the London School of Economics and an enthusiastic yoga instructor.

For more on climate and resilience: https://www.asiaswomenspeakers.com/lauren-sorkin

Getting Booked – How to get booked as a professional speaker

by Su-Yen Wong

Christmas shoppers clutched their festive purchases as they scurried along the sidewalk, eagerly headed to the next destination. As they approached the shiny shop window that fronted bustling Orchard Road at Robinsons—Singapore's oldest home-grown department store—they would invariably pause, if only momentarily, at the sight of a 15-year-old girl dressed in white, as part of the holiday display. She would perform seasonal favorites (think "Winter Wonderland" or a jazzed-up version of "Silent Night") on a white grand piano during the store's opening hours—some days up to 12 hours—to entertain passersby and draw them into the store.

Yes, I was that child, and this is what I consider to be my first professional gig. For my efforts, I was paid what was then (to me anyway) an eye-popping, four-figure sum. Being a musician is not too different from being a speaker. And I suspect my journey to becoming a professional speaker started right there in that showroom window.

I've since had the opportunity to help audiences in the United States, Asia, Europe, and Australia navigate the intersection of technology, strategy, and leadership. Here are nine lessons I've learned in that process about what it takes to get booked.

Be Relevant

While this may seem painfully obvious, getting booked requires having something compelling to say. This is the foundation upon which everything else gets built. So, what does it take to be relevant?

Understand the market context and client needs

As a professional speaker seeking to get booked, there are two important dimensions to understanding the market context and client needs.

The first is to stay connected with the latest trends and developments across a wide range of domains. The world we live in is changing at such a rapid pace that in order to remain relevant, it's important for me to have a well-tuned radar and and to constantly scan the horizon. This helps me make a link to the challenges and opportunities my audiences may be facing, and it equips me to draw out the implications for them.

Second, listen carefully to determine what underlying issue the client is trying to address. Two clients might approach me separately, each asking if I could deliver a session on "the future of work." While the answer in both cases might be affirmative, the reality is that the reasons they are looking for a speech on this topic could be vastly different. One might be keen to address a leadership gap, while the other might be interested in driving innovation.

Taken together, this is about being in a position to deliver maximum value to your clients. When I take the time to understand both their broad context and specific requirements, I have found clients far more receptive to confirming the booking. In my experience, clients very quickly pick up on whether or not you are both on the same wavelength!

Clarify your positioning

The next secret to getting booked is to craft your positioning as if you were a product, and then establish credibility in that space.

Don't agonize over someone else speaking about a similar topic as you. If you were designing a car, a computer, or a restaurant, you wouldn't worry about the fact that someone else has already designed a car/computer/restaurant, would you? Rather, you would probably think about which market and types of customers you are trying to serve, design your offering around that audience, focus on nurturing the right channels for that audience, and then go about developing a cult following in that space.

Being a professional speaker is no different, really. Your experience is unique, as are your stories. The critical path to getting booked is in determining your positioning or your niche, and in becoming known for it—especially with your target audience.

Keep evolving

So, you've worked on polishing your keynote speech for weeks on end. Your graphics look slick, and you have a repertoire of jokes that you have rehearsed to perfection. You know exactly when to pause for suspense, and for how long. Now what?

It's time to tweak and massage the message! When I was on the other side of the table and booking speakers, one of my top priorities in selecting a speaker was not just that she was a great speaker, but that she would be a great speaker *for my audience*. With this insight, I work hard as a speaker to customize and evolve my pitch so that it resonates with each and every audience. What does this mean in practice?

I am most frequently called upon to deliver keynote speeches on topics such as the future of work, leadership in an Asian century, and redesigning human capital. What I do is to engage in a fairly in-depth conversation with the client to gain an understanding of their pain points and objectives for the session. With this information in hand, I ensure relevance by adapting and evolving my speech specifically for that audience.

Back to a music or entertainment analogy, in a world that is characterized by short attention spans and audiences that are easily enticed by the next shiny new thing, I believe that artists with the greatest longevity (think Madonna or Michael Jackson) tend to be those with the willingness and ability to keep it fresh. So too, for us as speakers.

Get Out There

A market-relevant pitch notwithstanding, in order to get booked, you need to ensure potential clients are aware of how you can help their audiences or organizations. In other words, they need to know you exist! It's a wide, wide world... how does one go about this?

Work on people who have seen you in action

In his book *How to become a Global Keynote Speaker*, Fredrik Härén states emphatically, "The key to building a successful speaking career is a really great speech, which will lead to people booking you again."

I concur. The best source of new bookings is prior engagements. This almost sounds glib, but the truth is, there's no substitute for someone seeing you in action and deciding either to book you for a future event or to provide a referral to someone else. (Note: The converse is true as well—poor performances can certainly result in negative references!) Which is why every single audience engagement matters.

While many conference organizers earnestly pitch the benefits of "exposure," I've learned that most of the time it is an attempt to get speakers to reduce their fees or speak for free. Having said that, once in a while the forum may truly be a unique one that enables me to widen my reach with new audiences, thus increasing the likelihood of follow-on bookings. I like to think of such engagements as business development or brand-building activities. It's about making an investment that is expected to yield results.

Build presence and community

What's the next best thing to seeing you in action? Being aware that you are being booked by other people and staying close to the topics that are of interest.

Every speaker goes about increasing this awareness in a different way. For me, social media has played an important role in helping me stay connected with my community. I am most active on LinkedIn, as I've found this to be the most effective B2B channel. I know other speakers gravitate towards some combination of Facebook, Instagram, and Twitter.

What works for me are updates that keep people informed of upcoming events (particularly those that are public) where I will be speaking. Conference organizers tend to appreciate this too! Occasionally, I provide a bit of behind-the-scenes context or just-in-time commentary on the event itself. Lastly, I provide post-event recaps, that include other speakers and panelists, along with a brief summary of learning points from my session.

The bottom line is, don't expect people to automatically know about the great work you are doing! This kind of self-promotion may not feel natural at first, but as with anything else, practice makes perfect.

Engage with speaker bureaus

There are a variety of opinions on whether you should work with speaker bureaus or not. My perspective is that speaker bureaus can provide access to audiences to which you might not otherwise have had exposure. In my case, the ink was barely dry on our agreement when Priscilla Chan at Speakers Connect booked me for a keynote with a US-based association. This is not an opportunity that I would have uncovered on my own. I am perfectly happy to share a portion of my fee, and, furthermore, to send leads that come my way directly to her so that she can manage the client and all the other contractual details while I focus on honing my craft.

A final note on this: I believe that speaker bureaus, like executive search firms (or headhunters), generally want to be helpful to speakers. However, it's important to keep in mind that their first responsibility is to help their client fill a need. As a speaker, don't make the mistake of assuming that the speaker bureau's job is to help you get booked!

Play Nice

One of the great ironies of this day and age is that while the entire world is our oyster, it is also incredibly small in the sense that people are hyper-connected via social media and other means. What this implies for a speaker is that your reputation—as an individual—is something you must develop and protect.

Do good work

Delivering an excellent speech is the best thing I can do for a client who has put great trust in my ability to add value to the audience. At the end of the day, this is what matters—this is how reputations are built and how repeat bookings and referrals come about.

Be easy to work with

Conference organizers and corporate clients have many options to choose from. When I put myself in their shoes, I quickly appreciate that above and beyond a great speech, it's about inserting as little complexity as possible into their lives. Put simply, people must want to work with you. How do I translate this into specific actions on my part?

Upfront, I focus on understanding what clients are trying to accomplish, and I follow up promptly with any information they require, always keeping their deadlines in mind. On the day of the event, I get there ahead of time to check out the space and test the presentation. I also try my best to engage with the audience beforehand to get a sense of the overall mood. Sometimes this is about arriving earlier to observe prior sessions. If possible, I like to interact with participants during the tea break. Afterwards, and with the organizer's concurrence, I stick around for questions.

These are all small things. But taken together, they add up to make a difference to the client's overall impression and to increase the likelihood of subsequent bookings.

Help others

Always remember that the conference organizer, client, or speaker bureau has specific needs to be filled. Sometimes what I can offer is aligned with that need and other times it is not. Sometimes prior commitments preclude me from accepting a particular booking.

When faced with such situations, I try my best to connect the organizers to other speakers who may fit the bill. KeyNote Asia's Women Speakers is a perfect forum for this, and I have found organizers very receptive to such suggestions. They appreciate that you are trying to help them solve their issue, which creates goodwill for future opportunities. And it creates a virtuous circle with the speaker who is being recommended, who might be faced with a similar situation down the road and reciprocate with a referral.

Three Key Takeaways

Getting booked as a professional speaker boils down to three things:

- Be relevant
- Get out there
- Play nice

As women professional speakers we are, by default, role models on- and offstage for other women. The stories we tell and the experiences we share play an important role in shaping a balanced and holistic narrative in whichever domains we operate. I wish you much success in your journey as female professional speakers. Now, let the show begin!

Su-Yen Wong

Su-Yen Wong is founder and CEO of Bronze Phoenix, a premier provider of solutions that help organizations and leaders reinvent themselves. She is a thought leader and board director whose focus is the intersection of technology, strategy, and leadership.

Su-Yen is a highly-rated keynote speaker and guest lecturer at leading universities worldwide. She has advised some of the world's largest and most innovative and complex organizations, and she has been featured in media including *Bloomberg*, the *Wall Street Journal*, and the *Economist*.

Su-Yen serves on the boards of several public, private, and nonprofit organizations. In addition to an MBA, she holds a BA in music and computer science. She is an active member of Women Corporate Directors and the Young Presidents' Organisation.

For more on reinvention and the future of work: www.SuYenWong.com

Your Network is Your Net Worth

by Sonja Piontek

I've lived in Asia for more than ten years. Over the course of those beautiful, challenging, as well as highly rewarding years I've learned one thing in particular: the importance of *guanxi*, a little word with incredible significance.

Guanxi

Literally translated, guanxi (/gwanˈʃiː/, Chinese: 关系) means no more than "connection" or "relationship." The powerful Mandarin word, however, stands for so much more. It describes one of the central ideas in Chinese society, namely "the system of social networks and influential relationships which facilitate business and other dealings" *(Oxford Dictionary)*.

Given that I come from a Western background, it took me a while to fully understand and appreciate the concept of guanxi. "They promote nepotism?" I remember asking myself many years ago. Little did I know then that guanxi couldn't be further from the questionable practice of favoring relatives or friends. Today, my personal interpretation of guanxi is as follows: mutual empowerment and deep win-win relationships that are sustainably built and nourished over many, many years.

As with any other business, the business of professional speaking depends heavily on your relationships with the world out there. But let's not talk about the number of LinkedIn connections you have with potential clients that might consider you for a gig. They are important, no doubt. However, let us start with a much more profound aspect of guanxi, the concept of mutual empowerment.

Mutual Empowerment

When we talk about empowerment, one of the first things that often springs to mind is the idea of mentoring. Mentoring is an extremely powerful tool: finding a trusted partner who stands by your side, provides honest and valuable feedback, understands you, challenges you (oh yes, and I mean this in the most literal way), and helps you reach the next level.

On my journey to becoming a successful global keynote speaker, I've had the support of some remarkable mentors who triggered just the right thoughts when I most needed them. There was, for example, Lewis Pugh, UN Ambassador of the Oceans, Young Leader of the World, and one of the most compelling speakers I have ever met. In my former role as Director of Marketing for BMW Asia I booked Lewis as a speaker to inspire a crowd of over 4,000 clients during an impressive launch event spanning several days. When Lewis, whom I already knew from an event the previous year, arrived in Singapore, he asked me for a big favor: to give him clear feedback on his performance in order to help him improve his speaking and get "to the next level," as he so nicely worded it. I was deeply humbled by his trust. After all, he was one of the most inspiring speakers I had ever seen. But if he asked me, there had to be a reason why he thought I'd be the right person for the job. I said that it would be a great pleasure, but I added, "Just one thing. Do you want polite English feedback or honest German feedback?" With a smile on his face he opted for the latter, making a very wise choice that people often don't dare to make.

If you want to raise your game and truly excel, there is nothing better than honest feedback, even if it might hurt. The trick is to choose your mentors well. Base your relationship on trust, honesty, and respect. That way, even painful feedback will feel acceptable—especially as often it is the painful feedback that allows us to make the biggest leaps in our development.

Coming back to Lewis, I was thrilled to be able to support such an outstanding speaker in his quest to become even better at what he does. I gave it my best, my very best. We worked hard on his (already great) performance and indeed managed to bring it up another notch. Toward the end of the week, Lewis and I sat down on the sky terrace of the theatre where the event was held. By then, we had become close friends. Lewis looked deep into my eyes and said how thoroughly thankful he was for my support. The way he expressed his gratitude and worded his feedback deeply touched and profoundly inspired me. Though he had asked for *my* help at the beginning of the week, Lewis had become a mentor to me. In the end, without Lewis and his words of encouragement I would not have had the guts to leave BMW and the self-confidence to set up on my own company and become a global keynote speaker and entrepreneur.

This encounter can teach us an important universal truth: if you give from the bottom of your heart you will be rewarded manifold. Never would I have expected anything in return from Lewis. But by giving without demanding and by sharing without expecting, I got back much more than I could have ever asked for—the inspiration to start a new life!

Mutual empowerment has many faces and can happen in many ways. The essence is that you need to be willing to give before you ask to receive and that you find the right partners with whom you can mutually unleash your full potential and stimulate your strengths. As my current mentor and President of the APSS (Asia Professional Speakers Singapore) Fredrik Härén so passionately puts it, we are #BetterTogether.

Win-Win Relationships

I am often asked if I ever speak free of charge. Pro bono engagements aside, I would very clearly say no—despite the fact that I don't always get paid. How does that make sense—no payment and still not free of charge? Well, that's where the beauty of win-win relationships comes into play. Let me explain what I mean by sharing insights about a contract I recently signed with an international publishing house.

It all started when Stanley, their project manager, contacted me. They were in the midst of planning a pretty high-level global event for next year and they were keen to get me on stage to deliver the keynote speech. "Sweet," was my first thought, "that's a really nice one for my portfolio!" I was still available on the date and we discussed a suitable topic. It all seemed to be going great until Stanley uttered those destructive words that professional speakers really don't want to hear: "Sonja, we want you on board. I just need to honestly share that unfortunately we don't have the budget to pay your speaker fees."

To say that unfortunately I wouldn't be available would have been a fair reaction to Stanley's words. But when you've learned to appreciate the power of relationships and when you understand what it takes to build them, you'll understand why that's not what I said.

I am a true believer in win-win relationships and in crafting deals that benefit both parties. So, I took a deep breath and suggested, "How about we work on a barter deal that makes it worthwhile for both of us?"

Before I made this suggestion, I first reflected and confirmed that I was thoroughly interested in working with him. I really had a good feeling about Stanley, and I felt that he wasn't just trying to keep his expenses low; he seemed to genuinely be short on funds for the event. After talking back and forth, we settled for the following deal: I deliver the speech and in return he will do two features on me in his magazines—an agreement that I am quite happy with. Now, what is the moral of this story? Well, not only have I signed a high-profile speaking gig with two special PR features in highly relevant magazines as compensation, but more importantly have I established the foundation of a lasting relationship with Stanley—one that is based on mutual respect and trust. Who knows what business will continue to develop out of a relationship like this?

Another beautiful example of a win-win relationship combined with mutual empowerment is the friendship I've recently formed with fellow speaker Joanne Flinn. While she is clearly the "numbers brain" with an impressive executive career background, I am the "brand aficionado" with an understanding of all the professional tricks to build a premium brand. Whenever we meet we have fun, lots of fun, usually involving Nutella crêpes or something equally inappropriate. But we also share something else: every time we meet it's a very powerful exchange of knowledge and skills. Only last week, for example, were we sitting together to discuss the details of a rather big investment for my company, Sonnenkind Pte. Ltd. Joanne clearly knows more about this topic than I ever will. She helped me with valuable insights on even basic things like the right terminology. In that same session (after we had finished the crêpes) we also talked about her new Unicorn Coaching program. I was able to help her develop her new positioning as the Business Growth Lady. It really matches her personality. All in all, it was guanxi in action in the form of another lovely afternoon between friends, with great results on both sides. What a beautiful win-win relationship!

Many people say that you should never mix friendship and business. I totally disagree. During my corporate years I formed some of my deepest friendships with colleagues and business partners and it never harmed any of our projects—much to the contrary, I must say. Now that I run my own business, I only take onboard people that I appreciate not just for their business skills, but for their values and attitude. Some of my team have already been my friends for years, and with others I am just in the early stages of becoming friends. To me, life is much too valuable to spend it with people you don't have a good connection with.

The same goes for the international speaker community. Team up with those fellow speakers that you feel drawn to, who are on the same page as you. Don't see them as competition; rather see them as sparring partners that can stimulate you to soar. And allow friendship to happen, as it is the most beautiful basis for mutual empowerment and deep win-win relationships.

Time

Building a powerful network, like building a career as a professional speaker, does not happen overnight.

You can quickly add hundreds of connections on LinkedIn, join speaker foundations, go to events, exchange business cards, and do all sorts of things that will increase the number of contacts in your phone. But don't fool yourself with these numbers. In order to turn contacts into real connections, corporate titles into paying clients, acquaintances into friends, fellow speakers into trusted mentors, and names into meaningful relationships, a lot more has to happen and a lot of time and effort must be spent.

Never forget that trust is not something that happens immediately. It has to grow. Trust and a meaningful network need time and they grow best when you give before you demand. When you are genuine, authentic, openhearted, and kind, people will appreciate you, support you, and remember you. You will be able to build a successful and—more importantly—sustainable international speaker career.

> ## Three Key Takeaways
>
> My core message is simple:
>
> - Let the centuries-old concept of guanxi lead your way in your professional speaking career.
> - Focus on mutual empowerment and develop deep, win-win relationships.
> - Invest time and effort into building a sustainable network based on appreciation and trust.

And remember that to a great degree, your network is your net worth.

Sonja Piontek

Sonja Piontek is an award-winning international marketer and is often referred to by the press as "the Brand Aficionado." She recently left her position as Marketing Director for BMW Asia to set up her own company, www.sonnenkind.com.sg, a boutique agency creating unforgettable experiences for iconic brands such as Leica Camera, Land Rover as well as for companies in the private banking sector.

As a global keynote speaker, Sonja has inspired audiences across Asia and Europe alike. The passionate German speaks about "Creating Marketing Magic" or "Unleashing your Full Potential to Soar." Sonja and her work are regularly featured in business and luxury publications globally.

Originally from Munich, Sonja holds a master's degree in international business and culture studies, has lived in six countries, and speaks five languages.

For more on branding and soaring to your potential:
www.SonjaPiontek.com

Influential Negotiation – How to negotiate mutually beneficial speaking engagements

by Karen Leong

Have you ever stopped to consider why so many of us want to become keynote speakers? It is not just about the glamourous lifestyle. The fact is that each one of us is passionate about something. Each one of us has a message that we are eager to communicate, so it is not surprising that the number of people getting up on the stage increases exponentially every day. And this is good, because progress, development, and growth happen when more voices get heard and more ideas are exchanged.

The first thing I want to highlight is this passion. I am sure that you have heard a speaker who did everything perfectly right—textbook perfect in terms of the tone, the construction of the keynote, the gestures, and even the dress. Despite the fact that everything was spot on, the speaker failed to touch your heart. Have you wondered why?

And then there is the other kind of speaker who gets on stage and fumbles on so many fronts; yet this speaker brings an endearing authenticity, passion, and simplicity that move you deeply. Such a speaker is memorable and may even inspire you to action.

The lesson here is simple: passion and authenticity will always help you carry the day. Never lose sight of them. Harness them to put fire into your message.

And yes, you should augment their impact by employing some sensible techniques to make sure that your message gets the right branding and commercial appeal, so that it is heard far and wide and often. And at the right price. For money, though not everything, is important. It represents the value the market places on your message.

With this in mind, I want to share three things with you that I've learned over many years of fine-tuning our sales and client communication process at my company, Influence Solutions Pte. Ltd. (Influence Solutions). These three things have allowed us to better serve the client and have enabled us to deliver our best work. They will help ensure that you get the correct branding and also the right fiscal reward for all those hours of blood, sweat, and practice that you put into crafting each keynote.

Establish Your Value

My first tip is to establish your value before you allow your client to talk fees.

To do this effectively, you need to have clarity about the buying process that most clients employ when they are scouting for a keynote speaker. I'd like to highlight the three levels of communication that you can have with the buyer.

Level One — Inform

You will encounter buyers who have an event on a particular date and need a speaker within a certain budget. They may not express specific desired objectives beyond a general topic they'd like you to speak on. These clients are easily identified by the way they approach you, asking only for your availability on a particular date and requesting a quote.

If you respond directly to their questions, you are merely providing *information*. This is a classic Level One response. In most such cases, the buyer is using a "beauty pageant" approach and the price is usually the prime deciding factor. By affirming your availability and fee upfront, you miss the opportunity to expand on the value that you bring as a speaker and the impact you can create. Instead, you are likely to be viewed as a commodity, where the main differentiator is price and the lowest fee usually wins.

Level Two — Illustrate

You can easily shift this Level One buyer's focus to look beyond price when you help the buyer visualize the benefits they can reap by engaging you. That's you moving them to Level Two; where you *illustrate* your signature topics with the value they bring to the audience. By doing this you are enhancing your value, building your brand proposition, and helping the buyer to justify a higher fee investment in you. This approach can help bypass a lot of internal (and often unconscious) resistances and biases in the buyer.

Level Three — Influence

The key is to go one step further and elevate your response beyond Level Two to the third level, where you can most effectively influence the buyer. This happens when you establish your value, so that price is no longer the main determining factor. At this level, you shift the focus of the conversation to what's important to the buyer. Here you are helping to clarify the challenges they may be facing and establishing the importance of resolving them, hence positively reinforcing their return on investment.

Start by guiding the buyer to visualize how engaging you will help them achieve their desired goals, with outcomes such as enhancing engagement, boosting morale, inspiring change, and galvanizing action. This client-centric approach enables you to best position yourself as the catalyst in attaining the results they want. Notice how at Level Three you are no longer selling; rather you are a trusted partner, helping the client achieve a desired outcome.

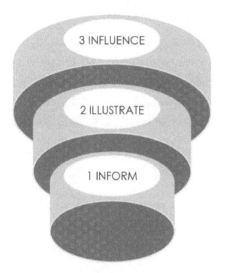

Level 3: INFLUENCE
You influence the buying decisions when you put the client first. You move from selling to helping the client buy you. You uncover top priorities and key challenges. By establishing yourself as the solution to their desired outcomes, price is no longer the main determining factor.

Level 2: ILLUSTRATE
You illustrate your signature topics and the value they bring to the audience. By building your brand proposition, it helps the buyer justify a higher investment with you.

Level 1: INFORM
You inform the buyer of your fee and availability. Price is often the prime deciding factor.

The three levels of influence

One example of this was when I was asked to deliver the opening keynote at the annual global sales conference of an MNC. The manager organizing the event approached me with some basic questions about my availability and cost. Instead of giving him that information (Level One), I uncovered the four main challenges they wanted to address. Then I shared how my keynote could be customized for their industry and to address two of the most common obstacles sales personnel from that industry faced. Not only did I land that engagement, I was also able to help the client realize the benefits of an additional closing keynote by my co-director, which would help cultivate a solutions-focused way of thinking in their sales team. The event went so well that this client has subsequently engaged our services for a series of speaking engagements as well as several training and coaching assignments.

So, let us look at some simple steps we can take to move the client from Level One to Level Three, and to ensure we are able to establish our value before we start talking price. This straightforward three-step process involves asking the client some very relevant questions, such as:

- What are two or three things you want from the event?
- What are the challenges that you face?
- What do you want to see people do differently after the keynote?

Please understand that this conversation is *very* important to every client. It enhances the possibilities they see in their event and sharpens their thinking about what they wish to achieve. So, spend time on this rather than jumping straight to the features and benefits of your keynote or how much you have been appreciated by other clients.

Once the client's needs have been clearly established and you've made it clear that your prime motive is to address those needs, then—and only then—you should share what you can do to curate and customize your keynote to meet these specific requirements.

And it is *only* when these two points have been discussed and firmed up that you start move on to the third step of talking about fees and other value-added options like books, online learning, and follow-up coaching.

Many speakers share with me that they only invest this kind of effort *after* they have been engaged. Perhaps this works for them. My experience has shown me that that offering value first helps secure the most beneficial and well-paid deals.

Does this work every time? Obviously not. It's business, not religion, and business decisions are influenced by many factors. That is why certain clients will still negotiate, despite your having done your best with this step. After all, it is the birthright of a client to negotiate and get the best value at the cheapest price. Whenever that happens, consider using my second tip.

Enhance Your Value Proposition

Tip number two is to enhance your value proposition instead of reducing the fee.

Whenever I am asked to reduce my fees, my first response is to counter by offering additional value and special bonuses. For example, I provide a copy of my book for every participant at a specially discounted price. This practice of including my book *Win People Over–75 Simple and Powerful Ways to Influence Anyone* as part of my keynotes helps enhance the overall experience for the audience, as well as providing a powerful credibility indicator.

Another value-added bonus I like to add, when I'm working on behalf of Influence Solutions, is a complimentary VIP pass package to the Rise Through the Ranks Summit™, our online leadership conference. These VIP passes give our clients' personnel unlimited access for one year to a fascinating collection of video interviews with forty global business and thought leaders from around the world.

Another example of demonstrating additional value is that if we notice that the keynote is part of a larger event or a series of regular events, we offer the buyer a special discount on a multiple-keynote package, encouraging them to take advantage of the various expert speakers at Influence Solutions.

Please remember that every negotiation is an opportunity to discover additional client needs, which could mean more speaking opportunities for you.

And again, no matter how well you do this, there will always be a client who wishes to negotiate even more. One way to respond to such endless negotiation is to decide what your fee threshold is and then decline to go below that. This is a smart business decision, because if clients suspect that you are willing to negotiate no matter what, you will find it very hard to get your speaking fees up to the level you want to command.

Offer a First-Engagement Discount

Another way forward is to employ my third tip, which is to demonstrate your value by offering a first-engagement discount.

This is a good way to let a new client experience the exceptional value that you can bring to their event and organization. At Influence Solutions, we are extremely confident of the value that our keynotes and programs have repeatedly delivered around the world. That is why we extend first-engagement discounts to new clients who have never experienced them before. This is also important because during keynotes we often get to engage senior decision-makers, or the actual beneficiary group.

No matter what stage you are at in your speaking business, you will benefit from expanding your sphere of influence when handling client negotiations. These three influential negotiation tips have not only enabled our teams at Influence Solutions to secure longer-term, six-figures client engagements, they have also provided us the opportunity to transform our impact and make a bigger difference.

Three Key Takeaways

To sum up, remember that your passion and message will only be heard when you:

- **establish value** before you talk fees;
- **enhance value** instead of reducing fees and in the ultimate scenario; and
- give a one-time, first-engagement discount to **demonstrate your value** so that you can actually command the speaking fee you deserve.

When you build a profitable speaking business you will be able to do what you love, make a positive difference, and expand your impact to the world.

Karen Leong

Karen Leong is a keynote speaker on transformation. A TEDx speaker and Certified Speaking Professional, Karen was featured in the ten most influential professional speakers in Singapore by the Singapore Business Review. Karen authored the best-seller *Win People Over*, and is the creator of the Influencing Styles profiling tool.

Karen is the managing director of Influence Solutions, a leading learning and development organization headquartered in Singapore, with offices in India and North America. As the co-founder Rise Through The Ranks™, a global online leadership summit, Karen has inspired thousands from over 70 countries.

A Women Icons awardee, Karen is regularly featured as an influence thought leader in global media such as BBC World, Reuters, Channel News Asia and The Straits Times. She is a sought-after expert commentator for iconic events such as the USA presidential debates and the Trump-Kim summits.

For more on influence and transformation: www.karenleong.com

The Dollars and Sense of Speaking Professionally

by Dr. Indigo Triplett

How would you like to discover alternative financial paths while pursuing your passion? Let's start by exploring a few questions. Is speaking a pastime hobby for you? Do you have a "job," and is speaking an opportunity for you to represent the organization that pays your salary? Are you a practitioner earning your livelihood on the stage? Do you speak as a way to generate business for a different revenue stream, such as being a consultant, author, or coach? Perhaps you are a hybrid combining two or more of the above paths to professional speaking. Whatever the case, you need to be clear of your business model, because that will drive your rates and expectations.

To use myself as an example, I don't market myself as a speaker per se, but rather as a businesswoman who speaks. Though I am paid to pick up the mic, I don't earn my living primarily through speaking. I follow the many professional practices of a professional speaker, and the stage gives me access to potential buyers.

Be clear on your business model—in other words, why you are speaking. If you are doing it for fun and amusement, you're going to have a hard time convincing buyers to hire you over a professional. This chapter is for people who want to be a professional in this business.

I liken the speaking business to fast food chains. Some conference organizers ask anyone to speak: employees of brand-name companies, or people who know someone important but who are not necessarily an expert. Let's call them McDonald's. It has a little of everything, from burgers to chicken. Other organizers who want specialized speakers are willing to pay because they want professionals who are experts and have honed their craft. Let's call them KFC. Both have chicken, but one *specializes* in chicken, and that is where you will see more of an appreciation for professional speakers. Do you want to be the everything speaker to everyone (McDonalds), or do you want to be the specialized speaker with a specific audience (KFC)? Your answer to this question is the foundation of your business model.

Once you know your objective for speaking, you must develop tools that will bring credibility. Some people believe credibility is in your licensing, experience, education, and titles. I believe credibility is what you are able to demonstrate to get invited to the stage. I turned an important corner in my speaking career when I published my book, started writing articles, and became a columnist in magazines. This isn't as difficult as it may seem. There are so many media outlets clamoring for relevant and top-shelf material to attract an audience. You could write for a newsletter in your company, be a contributor or columnist for a magazine in your industry, or blog. Blogging is what I do these days, merely because I enjoy it and I want to speak in my most authentic voice. Writing for national magazines required writing for the personality of the magazine and its audience, but this served its purpose and propelled my speaking career. While it's beneficial when others write about you, you cannot necessarily control what they'll say. On the other hand, you have complete control over what you write and what you get out to the masses.

If you have enough materials and a message that you can elaborate upon at length, then you are ready for a book. That, in my opinion, is the ultimate game-changer. Writing several books has allowed me to capture my message and then lift out excerpts that demonstrate my expertise to potential clients. The greatest benefit is that I'm able to sell those books at speaking engagements and around the world. Your books can earn money on their own while leading to paid engagements.

Getting the Gig

As women, we often don't have a healthy appreciation for money. Over a year ago, a colleague put me in touch with a potential client. She went as far as setting up a dinner meeting and accompanying me to introduce me to her contact. I told her that I would give her a finder's fee. She said alright, waving her hand with a dismissive gesture. A couple of months later, I got a contract. I told her again that I would give her a finder's fee. And again, her response was along the lines of, "Yeah, whatever." Ninety days after delivery, I contacted her to give her 10% of the profits. She was shocked and said that I was giving her too much. I laughed and said, "You are right, but I appreciate what you did more than you'll ever know." When we met up and I tried to put the cash in her hands, she refused to accept the entire amount and gave me back some of the money.

There are several things I want you to take away from this example:

1. Ask people to introduce you into their network but be very clear about what your sweet spot is and what you want to speak on. People often make the mistake of recommending you for things that don't align with your platform and then you feel obligated

to deliver. This will not serve you well, and it may even hurt your reputation.

2. Do what you say you will do. If you tell someone that you will introduce them to a decision-maker, keep your word. If you are uncomfortable allowing people to have access to your network, then don't offer it up.

3. Pay finder's fees. I have done this since I started my first company in 1995, and I'm amazed how many people work under the guise of "favors." This is a business, and professionals pay and get paid. When someone brokers or intercedes on your behalf, that is marketing. I look at referrals as an important part of my business development and I'm willing to pay for them. The exchange of money or services shows value and appreciation.

4. If you offer to pay someone a finder's fee, then have integrity and pay them as soon as you are paid. Earmark that money as business development and even include it in your overall cost of doing business, if need be. But do it.

Dollars and Sense

Be clear on whether or not there is a budget, even if you are referred by someone. Recently, a professional told me about a conference with "big-name" speakers. She asked whether I wanted in. She explained that I wouldn't be paid. I replied that the big-name men would be paid, right? When I declined, she said that I must not need opportunities. No. I'm just not desperate, and I value myself and what I have to offer. It would have cost me money in terms of time as well as the expense of travel and shipping books. Also, that audience was not necessarily my audience, so I had nothing to gain. It is imperative you do the math on your expenses along with the possible return on your investment.

Here's an easy equation that I use when coaching clients. Brainstorm the following: (1) what will you gain if you do this speaking opportunity, and (2) what will you lose if you do not do this engagement? Ask yourself, (3) what are the risks and benefits if you push the envelope to be paid? Only you can determine the validity of your responses. So, answer these questions and reflect on what you have written. It will begin to make *sense*. Then you'll know what to do regarding accepting or rejecting an offer to speak.

Getting Paid Takes Courage

I have found in Asia that there is not a healthy appreciation or value for paid speakers. Conference planners often have the audacity to ask me to pay to speak, even though they are charging attendees. Yeah, *nah*! I've come to expect it, but I don't accept it. There are organizers who want experts and will compensate fairly. I'm a professional speaker and if that conference planner is getting paid, I need to be paid as well. I understand the rationale that certain speakers are paid by their companies because it is good marketing for them, but if you are not attached to an organization that will foot your expenses, be careful of taking on assignments that will cost you. Arrive at a range that you believe reflects your value, what the market will bear, and quite simply, what you need to earn case by case.

I will occasionally speak for free based on a relationship, the mission of the organization, or other factors that promise a value or benefit for me. If you choose to speak gratis, be very clear on what you will gain. If the organization legitimately cannot pay you, negotiate something of value from them such as a letter of recommendation, at least three viable introductions within their network or organization, or extended travel/accommodations for you to take advantage of the trip. I'll say more later about negotiating a value exchange, but the important piece is that you must ask for compensation. You will receive what you believe you are worth, and you will receive nothing if you are unwilling to ask.

Recently, I was coaching someone about asking for what she wanted. She held her chest, while shaking her head no, and said, "I can't do that." I asked her to write down and repeat the following: *I need my money more than they need my money.* Once she had repeated that phrase a few times, it made sense to her. As a professional speaker, you are accountable for what you do or do not receive. The pay gap between men and women is less about policy than our inability to negotiate and ask for what we deserve! Take ownership of what you want for yourself.

Whenever an organizer tries to give me the ole' party line about not having a budget to pay speakers, I ask several questions to gain courage. You can use them to analyze the situation before accepting an opportunity:

(1) Is the person asking me to speak for free doing their job for free? If it is truly a nonprofit organization staffed by volunteers, then they probably are. But if it is a company or NGO, that person earns a salary and is being paid. Would they show up to work for free the way they're asking you to?

(2) Are they unable or just unwilling to pay? Try to look at both angles. If you ask about the agenda and a review of their past events clearly shows that they have a budget to offer an expensive menu, rent a premier venue, and pay everyone including the servers, will you be okay with not being paid? If this were musical chairs, would you be the only person without a chair? If everyone is being paid but you, shame on you for accepting to deliver your services.

(3) Who will gain what from your presentation? If you are truly delivering knowledge to their clients or employees, that has a price! Delivering to executives should be a different rate than speaking to high school students, right? You must prepare your slides and notes, take time off for travel, and so forth. Expectations will differ based on your audience and the size of the group, so use these considerations to help you formulate your price.

You must have the courage to ask these questions and to walk away, if necessary. When people sense that you will speak for free and that you want the opportunity more than they need you, they will leverage that and take advantage of you and your talents. Don't take the "it's good marketing" bait. Have the courage to say, "Thank you, but I'm unable to accept your offer. I can refer you to someone who would be interested in working with your terms or budget, but I'm a professional speaker with overhead." I then share the opportunity with whomever I have in mind and allow them to contact the organizer; I don't hesitate to pass on such opportunities to someone else who may benefit from that gig for reasons other than money.

Free work begets free work, and cheap people know cheap people. Organizers who don't pay will refer you and will mention that you worked for free, and so the next person will expect not to pay you. It's a vicious cycle. But when they pay and refer you, they will mention that you were worth your fee, and the next organizer will be less likely to ask you to work for free.

Help Your Client Compensate You

The business of professional speaking is first and foremost, a career, profession or job. I have found the best way to manage your career as a speaker is to recognize these different avenues to take in pursuing your passion. For instance: (1) is it a past-time hobby for you, (2) do you have a 'job' and is speaking an opportunity as you represent an organization that pays your salary, (3) are you a practitioner who earns your livelihood on the stage, (4) do you speak as a way to generate business for a different revenue stream such as consultant, author, coach, etc. and (5) is there a hybrid of two aspects? You need to be clear of your business model because that will drive your rates and expectations.

When quoting your rate, ask these questions to make sure you give a fair, reasonable and competitive price: (1) Who are the audience members? Are they staff, leaders, volunteers, millennials, etc.? (2) How long will you speak and in what time slot? This tells you how much you must prepare. Opening and closing are usually the toughest slots, requiring you either to lay an exciting foundation for the day or to close it out in a way that satisfies everyone. (3) What is the nature of the event? Is it mandatory, celebratory, expertise based, etc.? (4) Will you be on the mainstage or in breakout sessions? This will help you to anticipate the audience size and room format. (5) What is their budget for speakers? These are just a few things that I take into consideration to prevent being blindsided and to calibrate my price.

But I also recognize that compensation doesn't always mean money: it's about what is a value exchange. When I served on boards and committees, I would approach organizations to get donations. You will be surprised how many companies need to give charitable donations or other things of value. For example, Coca Cola would give me pallets of products that I would in turn gift to parks. So, barter and negotiate and show your clients how they can compensate you.

Ask the client about their relationships with other venues, media outlets, airlines, or other companies that are of interest to you. It may be membership to a golf club to further your networking, or a set number of all-inclusive nights at a resort or hotel that you frequent for business travel. They can approach those companies where they have relationships and ask for ways to compensate you. For example, just recently a client negotiated to have me featured in a magazine. This was a win-win deal for all involved. The client was able to receive a service without a direct cash expense, the magazine got some quality content, and I received compensation via exposure.

There are countless things that can be requested, bartered for, and granted. If clients ask what's in it for the companies they are approaching, tell them that in exchange for their gifts, they can list donor companies in the conference brochure. Such gifts will result in free advertising, not to mention potential new clients among the recipients of the gifts.

If you accept the offer to speak get everything in writing, even if it is gratis. Make sure to include travel expenses, invoicing, and follow-up expectations. I have a Memorandum of Understanding that I send to make sure both parties are on the same page and that expectations on each side are clear.

You may have to think outside of the box to get compensated, but the important thing is a transaction that shows a value exchange. If you are unwilling to ask for it, you may not deserve to be compensated. And if they are unwilling to do something for you, then they may not deserve you.

What's Next

After you've delivered and exceeded their expectations, it's time to start laying a foundation for the next opportunity to speak. Follow up with clients and with all the business cards you will collect. I give a copy of my book to the client as a thank you for their business and support. I also request a letter of recommendation or a copy of the evaluations. You may want to post the many pictures that will be taken and get quotes from attendees to include in future proposals.

Giving of Yourself

Your book should be an extension of you and your message. It allows you to up-sell your presentation, before and after. I often use my book as a bargaining chip; for instance, if there is no budget to pay me as a speaker, is there a budget for books? Often my clients pay *and* buy books. When you touch your audience they will want a piece of you, and one way to give that to them is through your book(s).

Why Letters?

When you contact your client and thank them for the opportunity to speak or be of service, ask for a letter of recommendation that you can share with potential clients. I ask for a variety of letters with different elements. For instance, I may ask one client to discuss my style because someone may be on the fence about hiring me if they don't know whether my style will fit their audience. I may ask a different organizer for a letter speaking about my ability to work closely with them or their team. If I want to showcase versatility in clients who have hired me, I may ask prestigious clients to write something. I include two or three such letters whenever I send my proposal.

These few things have led to great success for me. If my advice resonates with you, I hope you will embrace it, own it, and run with it. Not everything works for everyone, but I hope you can glean something that will move you to the next level of your speaking career.

Three Key Takeaways

- Building a business takes grit and determination, and being a speaker is a business with you and your message as the product.
- Know why you are speaking. What role does speaking play in your business model?
- Have the courage to treat this as a business proposition. Be savvy about going further and using your books and letters of recommendation to connect with new clients.

Dr. Indigo Triplett

Dr. Indigo Triplett has successfully owned and operated a multimillion-dollar HR consulting firm that she established in 1995 in the US. She and her career sustainability philosophy have been featured in *INC Magazine, Ebony,* Fox News, the *New York Times, Huffington Post, Femina* and many other media outlets. Her book series *Playing by the Unwritten Rules* is the foundation of her signature presentations and keynotes. In addition to leading her company, she uses her international experience and research to help organizations grow, through talent management, and to compete in the "glocal" (global/local) market. Her PhD in values-driven leadership has positioned her to help individuals and leaders become more effective, both personally and professionally, in seeking greater profitability and career sustainability.

For more on business and personal purpose: www.4-DPerformance.com

Where It All Began

by Aurelie Saada and Mette Johannson

Coffees and ideas brewed, then pancakes and plans were put on the table over brunch. Seven of us met with a joint vision to make the playing field more equal and bring diversity to stages around the world.

One of our ideas was this book. Only nine months later, it's in your hands. We hope it helps you bring your career, business, and vision to new levels.

On speaking stages, whether at conferences, events, or corporate gatherings, it's frequently men only. Even in Singapore, a truly blended society in terms of race, the stage is not only dominated by men but also by men with homogenous racial origins.

We are changing this. You are changing this. This book is part of the change.

The public speaking tradition is at a tipping point

Since antiquity, the norm was for women to be silent in public In Confucian China, homes were divided into an inner and outer section. Women were to stay in the inner section and were forbidden to speak in public. Christianity traditionally distinguished where women's voices were desired: in private, not in public. We were to be seen and not heard.

If you search for the ten greatest speeches in American history, you will not find a single woman's name. Even in the 20th century, society's bias saw men as more trustworthy subject-matter experts.

Today, we're at a tipping point.

TED Talks, the new standard for public speaking, shows this. Currently, 10 out of the 25 most-watched TED speakers are women, even though the majority of proposed speakers are male. Nobody forces you to watch a TED Talk. People *choose* to watch women speakers even though they are in a minority. Our conclusion? People want to watch women speakers. Women speakers can be as formidable and inspiring as men.

We are truly at the tipping point to make public speaking a more diverse undertaking and profession.

For society as a whole, this is a welcome development. Diversity results in higher group intelligence and increased creativity. For women, it's an opportunity to take a big step towards equality. We're convinced that more women speaking in public will result in a ripple effect to other parts of society including academia, business, and government. By speaking up and by listening to more women on stages, we recognize and respect female thought leaders and women leaders in general.

We seven women are all part of a nonprofit association to help women excel. We created a directory for female speakers, and we refer male speakers, too. We are inclusive. What's more, top male speakers have pledged their support to us. They, too, know that with greater diversity on stage everybody wins. When pledging their support for diversity, some men even say they would refuse to be part of an all-male panel or speaker lineup. These men stand with their strong wives and especially their daughters, for whom they wish to see an equal future.

PrimeTime and KeyNote

PrimeTime is a professional and business women's association in Singapore. We launched KeyNote, Asia's only (and hence leading) directory of women speakers in December 2017.

The idea behind KeyNote was simple. We were tired of all-male conferences and panels ("manels"). We wanted to do something about #wherearethewomen. Our goal was to make it easier for conference organizers to find accomplished women speakers, and so the directory was born.

KeyNote Women Speakers has the simple mission of bringing diversity to stages around Asia. This soon turned into a more ambitious mission of bringing diversity to stages around the world as our message spread to Europe and the US.

From the directory, the idea grew to include a training program for women who want to improve their public speaking skills. As professional speakers ourselves, we know that there are special considerations for women speakers. We saw that one strength in our KeyNote training program was that the women were being trained by women professional speakers.

Our activities focus on three pillars:

- Giving women speakers more visibility
- Training the NextGen of female speakers
- Providing conference owners, associations, and other organizations easy access to a high-quality and diverse body of speakers

This book has been created in the spirit of PrimeTime's raison d'être: women empowering women to reach their highest potential. It's packed with insight, impact, and inspiration for women to find the inner strength to speak out and express their ideas. We hope you enjoy putting it all into action.

We hope this book will give you the confidence, mindset, and skillset, so that—no matter your gender, race, religion, or ability—you can and will speak up, on stages around the world, but also at work and in your private lives.

Aurelie Saada, President, PrimeTime Business and Professional Women's Organization

Mette Johansson, Chair, KeyNote Women Speakers directory